RISING STARS Spelling

Teacher's Guide
Spelling activities for every week

Gill Matthews

Year 3

Every effort has been made to trace all copyright holders, but if any have been inadvertently overlooked, the Publishers will be pleased to make the necessary arrangements at the first opportunity.

Although every effort has been made to ensure that website addresses are correct at time of going to press, Rising Stars cannot be held responsible for the content of any website mentioned in this book. It is sometimes possible to find a relocated web page by typing in the address of the home page for a website in the URL window of your browser.

Hachette UK's policy is to use papers that are natural, renewable and recyclable products and made from wood grown in sustainable forests. The logging and manufacturing processes are expected to conform to the environmental regulations of the country of origin.

ISBN: 978-1-47187-926-5

Text, design and layout © 2016 Rising Stars UK Ltd
First published in 2016 by Rising Stars UK Ltd
Rising Stars UK Ltd, part of Hodder Education Group
An Hachette UK Company
Carmelite House 50 Victoria Embankment London EC4Y 0DZ
www.risingstars-uk.com
All facts are correct at time of going to press.

Author: Gill Matthews
Educational Consultant: Pauline Allen
Publisher: Laura White
Illustrator: Gillian Flint c/o Bright Educational
Logo design: Julie Martin
Design: Julie Martin
Typesetting: York Publishing Solutions
Cover design: Julie Martin
Project Manager: Haremi Ltd.
Copy Editor: Melanie Gray
Proofreader: Jennie Clifford

All rights reserved. Apart from any use permitted under UK copyright law, no part of this publication may be reproduced or transmitted in any form or by any means, electronic or mechanical, including photocopying and recording, or held within any information storage and retrieval system, without permission in writing from the publisher or under licence from the Copyright Licensing Agency Limited. Further details of such licences (for reprographic reproduction) may be obtained from the Copyright Licensing Agency Limited, Barnard's Inn, 86 Fetter Lane, London EC4A 1EN.

Pages that can be photocopied are clearly marked at the bottom of each page. The rights of Gill Matthews to be identified as the author of this work have been asserted by her in accordance with the Copyright, Design and Patents Act 1998.

British Library Cataloguing-in-Publication Data A CIP record for this book is available from the British Library.
Printed by Ashford Colour Press Ltd.

MIX
Paper from responsible sources
FSC® C011748

Contents

Autumn term

How does 'happy' become 'happier'?	8
Focus: review of Year 2 suffixes (-ed, -ing, -er and -est)	
How does 'beauty' become 'beautiful'?	10
Focus: review of Year 2 suffixes (-ness, -ment, -ful, -less)	
Can we spell words from our word list?	12
Focus: words from the Year 3/4 word list	
How do we spell the /i/ sound in words?	14
Focus: the /i/ sound spelled with a 'y'	
How can we spell the /u/ sound in words?	16
Focus: the /u/ sound spelled 'ou'	
Can you correct your own writing?	18
Focus: words from children's own writing	
How can we spell the /ai/ sound?	20
Focus: the /ai/ sound spelled 'ei', 'eigh' or 'ey'	
How can we use prefixes?	22
Focus: the un-, dis- and mis- prefixes	
When do we double the consonant?	24
Focus: adding suffixes	
How can we spell long vowel sounds?	26
Focus: spelling split digraphs	
Can we spell words from our word list?	28
Focus: words from the Year 3/4 word list	
Can you correct your own writing?	30
Focus: words from children's own writing	

Spring term

Who will win the spelling quiz?	32
Focus: review of Autumn term spellings	
Who will win the revision quiz?	34
Focus: review of Autumn term spellings	
Can we spell words from our word list?	36
Focus: words from the Year 3/4 word list	
How can we use prefixes?	38
Focus: the prefix re-	
Can we make our spelling super?	40
Focus: prefixes super-	
Can you correct your own writing?	42
Focus: words from children's own writing	

How can we use prefixes?	44
Focus: the prefixes anti- and sub-	
How can we use prefixes?	46
Focus: prefix auto-	
How can we use prefixes?	48
Focus: prefix inter-	
What are homophones?	50
Focus: homophones and near-homophones	
Can we spell words from our word list?	52
Focus: words from the Year 3/4 word list	
Can you correct your own writing?	54
Focus: words from children's own writing	

Summer term

Who will win the spelling quiz?	56
Focus: review of Spring term spellings	
Who will win the spelling quiz?	58
Focus: review of Spring term spellings	
Who can remember the word list?	60
Focus: words from the Year 3/4 word list	
How does 'happy' become 'happily'?	62
Focus: the -ly suffix	
How does 'simple' become 'simply'?	64
Focus: the -ly suffix	
Can you correct your own writing?	66
Focus: words from children's own writing	
How does 'basic' become 'basically'?	68
Focus: suffixes -ally and -ation	
How does 'control' become 'controlled'?	70
Focus: suffixes (vowel letters)	
How does 'confuse' become 'confusion'?	72
Focus: -sion and -tion endings	
How does 'active' become 'inactive'?	74
Focus: in- and il- prefixes	
How does 'possible' become 'impossible'?	76
Focus: im- and ir- prefixes	
Who can remember the word list?	78
Focus: review of Year 3 words from the Year 3/4 word list	

Statutory Word List for Year 3 and 4
Grouped by possible teaching areas

suffix -ly, -ally (year 3)	accidentally, actually, occasion(ally), probably
-tion and -sion words (year 3)	position, possess(ion), question, mention, occasion
split digraph – long vowel sounds (year 3) — Two letters split across a word make one sound (e.g. guide – i–e)	extreme, guide, describe, decide, surprise, arrive *(review work from year 1)*
/n/ spelled as 'kn' (year 4)	knowledge, knowledgeable
/or/ sound spelled 'augh' (year 3)	caught, naughty
/ai/ sound spelled 'ei', 'ey' and 'eigh' (year 3)	eight/eighth, reign, weight, height *(exception)*
cross-curricular words (year 3 and 4)	earth, eight/eighth, fruit, heart, history, increase, minute, natural, opposite, position, quarter, regular, weight
adverbials (year 4)	therefore
-ous words (year 4)	famous, various
-ible words (year 4)	possible
/s/ sound spelled 'c' before 'e', 'i' and 'y' (year 4)	centre, century, certain, circle, consider, bicycle, decide, exercise, experience, medicine, notice, recent *(review work from year 2)*
-ough letter strings (year 4)	enough, though/although, thought, through *(currently taught in year 5/6)*
words from other countries (year 3 and 4)	bicycle
double consonants (year 3)	address, appear, arrive, difficult, grammar, suppose, opposite, pressure, occasion, disappear, different
/i/ sound spelled 'u' (year 3)	busy/business
adding prefixes and suffixes (year 3)	(re)build, (dis)believe, (dis)appear, (re)position
unstressed vowels (year 4)	library, February, ordinary, separate, different, favourite, interest
other words (year 3 and 4)	answer, breath, breathe, build, calendar, complete, continue, early, earth, experiment, group, guard, forward(s), fruit, heard, heart, history, imagine, increase, important, island, learn, length, material, minute, natural, often, particular, peculiar, perhaps, popular, potatoes, promise, purpose, quarter, remember, regular, sentence, special (-tial words), straight, strange, strength, surprise, woman/women

YEAR 3, SPELLING PLANNING OVERVIEW

	Autumn 1	Autumn 2	Spring 1	Spring 2	Summer 1	Summer 2
Week 1	**Focus:** review of Year 2 suffixes (-ed, -ing, -er and -est)	**Focus:** the /ai/ sound spelled 'ei', 'eigh' or 'ey'	**Focus:** review of Autumn term spellings	**Focus:** the prefixes anti- and sub-	**Focus:** review of Spring term spellings	**Focus:** suffixes -ally and -ation
Week 2	**Focus:** review of Year 2 suffixes (-ness, -ment, -ful, -less)	**Focus:** the un-, dis- and mis- prefixes	**Focus:** review of Autumn term spellings	**Focus:** prefix auto-	**Focus:** review of Spring term spellings	**Focus:** suffixes (vowel letters)
Week 3	**Focus:** words from the Year 3/4 word list	**Focus:** adding suffixes	**Focus:** words from the Year 3/4 word list	**Focus:** prefix inter-	**Focus:** words from the Year 3/4 word list	**Focus:** -sion and -tion endings
Week 4	**Focus:** the /i/ sound spelled with a 'y'	**Focus:** spelling split digraphs	**Focus:** the prefix re-	**Focus:** homophones and near-homophones	**Focus:** the -ly suffix	**Focus:** in- and il- prefixes
Week 5	**Focus:** the /u/ sound spelled 'ou'	**Focus:** words from the Year 3/4 word list	**Focus:** prefix super-	**Focus:** words from the Year 3/4 word list	**Focus:** the -ly suffix	**Focus:** im- and ir- prefixes
Week 6	**Focus:** words from children's own writing	**Focus:** words from children's own writing	**Focus:** words from children's own writing	**Focus:** words from children's own writing	**Focus:** words from children's own writing	**Focus:** review of Year 3 words from the Year 3/4 word list

Introduction

The aim of this book is to provide some practical and exciting ways to teach spelling within the classroom. The teaching sequence closely follows the national curriculum 2014. Some of the sounds to be taught have been combined within one week's teaching to enable the entire year group's curriculum to be fully covered. Each unit (which takes up a double page within the book) shows roughly a week's worth of teaching. This might all be taught in one session or broken up over different sessions (including work at home). This is open to the teacher's discretion.

Effective spelling strategies

As part of a spelling programme different strategies need to be used to enable each individual learner to access the curriculum. Throughout the book, ideas are provided as to how to teach in a variety of styles, giving written, practical and oral activities. Learning spelling strategies is an individual process, and giving children different means by which to learn will enable them to choose an appropriate method which works for them. Effective spelling strategies should include a combination of reading and writing, together with quality teaching. This book should be used in conjunction with an individual school spelling policy to ensure that a variety of methods are used.

The primary strategies that are utilised in the teaching sequences in this book are:

- **Phonetic spelling strategies:** Awareness of phonetics is the most common method used to teach spellings, using individual phonemes representing letters together with a combination of digraphs and trigraphs representing groups of letters. Using segmenting and blending skills as part of this strategy is crucial. This is effective for most children; however awareness of common exception words that do not fit into a phonetic strategy is essential to work alongside this strategy. This strategy is the most useful basis for early spelling and is a primary focus in KS1. As children move through education, into KS2 and beyond, it is important that they have this foundation on which they can build a more extensive strategic approach.
- **Visual spelling strategy:** Some learners find this method key to successful learning. Learning how a word looks and visualising the word can be extremely effective. This can prove useful for all learners, especially with the trickier common exception words and with homophones, being able to distinguish when a word looks correct written down.
- **Mnemonics:** This method is useful in giving children a memory device by which to learn the spelling pattern of a specific word. Whilst this is useful, it does have a limitation in the number of rhymes that a child can successfully remember to be able to regularly apply this method.
- **Rule-based strategies:** Throughout the book a number of rules are provided to help give children an understanding of the theory behind spelling patterns. Understanding syllables and rules surrounding patterns can also help children learn.
- **Word-meaning strategies:** Helping children understand what words mean can support their spelling of those words. Explaining how words are derived, how prefixes and suffixes are added on to root words and how to form abbreviations and compound words, can all support confidence and accurate spelling.

Teaching a range of strategies is essential so that some of these strategies become automatic and instinctive for learners in their work.

Teaching techniques

This book aims to provide a range of teaching techniques. Children need to see confident, accurate spelling modelled using the strategies outlined above. A range of activities are provided, such as:

- **Written activities:** Look, say, cover, write, check is a well-established way of learning spellings. In this book it has been used in a variety of ways. It is important to teach children to proofread or check their work. By giving children a modelled form of the word or sentence with which to compare their work, we can teach them to identify their errors by themselves or with support from a peer. Having done this we can further teach them to edit their spelling, thereby hopefully embedding the correct form. Encouraging children to have the confidence to attempt challenging spellings and not be afraid to try is key to progression in spelling. Dictation has also been used as a form of reviewing the quality of teaching and learning.

- **Oral activities:** It is useful for children to be able to learn spelling in oral activities. This enables words to be put into context and ensures the correct use of the words. Use of sound buttons, robot arms, chop and stretch, and other methods are helpful when learning to read and spell words. Encouraging children to be creative in sentence construction is also useful so that learned spellings are put into context whilst helping them to enjoy learning to spell.
- **Games:** These have been widely used within the book to encourage children to learn whilst they play. The games are generally followed by a different form of activity to further embed the learning. Targeted use of colouring in the identification of correct spellings and misspellings is a useful method to engage the learner and has been used in a range of ways in the activities.
- **Stories and rhymes:** These are used in the book to grab the attention of the listeners, encouraging them to spot sounds and make links with spelling patterns.

Ensuring good spelling in writing

Learners need to understand that words are made up of individual sounds (or phonemes). Once they have understood this they need to be given the opportunity to manipulate the sounds to make blended sounds and words. Only then can the process of decoding and encoding begin. For effective reading, learners need to decode using phonemic knowledge together with a range of other strategies to deal with exception words. For the process of writing, learners need to understand the converse approach – that of encoding individual phonemes. Good teaching will encourage children to manipulate sounds, practising encoding strategies whilst using the spelling principles taught. Modelling good spelling practices (e.g. within a shared or modelled writing task) is essential to encourage learners to apply the principles. Learners should also develop the use of dictionaries and other tools to check their spelling and to realise when there are word and spelling choices.

Good writers should draw on a range of spelling strategies in their work, such as:
- recalling words from memory.
- using sound-letter and phoneme knowledge to work out words.
- using knowledge of root words, prefixes and suffixes.
- using spelling rules and conventions.
- trial and error/visualisation – writing the word to check if it looks right.
- linking known words or parts of words.
- using supporting materials, such as dictionaries, phoneme mats and alphabet code charts.
- using spelling journals as an aide memoire.

This book aims to help children use good spelling in their writing using all these different strategies. At a suitable juncture after children have written a word or sentence, teachers need to encourage them to review it, proofread it and edit it if necessary. A suggested stepped approach is as follows:
- Initially ask the children to say the word they have written in its entirety.
- Secondly, the children need to be asked to decode the word they have written phonetically, if possible.
- Then ask the children to blend the sounds and say the word that they have written.
- Where the word is not phonetically decodable they need to be reminded to use one of the other strategies they have been taught (e.g. visualisation, recalling from memory, use of phoneme mats) to check if they think the word is spelled correctly.
- They should be asked if the word they have written is the word they intended, or have they created a different word.
- If they think the word is not what they intended, they should be encouraged to change it. A positive approach here is essential so as to preserve self-esteem and encourage them to try again.
- Young children can initially struggle to correct individual letters within words and it is often easier to ask them to cross out the whole word and try again. As children develop self-esteem in their ability to spell, they can be encouraged to correct letters within words.
- Finally, it is often helpful for children to ask a peer to read their work and check that what they have read is what they intended to write.

How does 'happy' become 'happier'?

Focus: review of Year 2 suffixes (-*ed*, -*ing*, -*er* and -*est*)

You will need:
Access online resources at My Rising Stars: www.risingstars-uk.com
- A4 whiteboards and pens
- Suffix cards
- Ted, the Tiny Bear resource per pair
- Dictionaries

In a nutshell

Teacher subject knowledge for this unit:

This unit reviews year 2 suffixes work on adding -*ed*, -*ing*, -*er* and -*est*. When words end in 'y', the 'y' changes to an 'i' when the suffixes -*er* and -*est* are added. When a word ends in 'e', the 'e' at the end of the word is dropped when the suffixes -*er*, -*ing* and -*ed* are added.

Word list

happier	hiking	fluffiest	cute	copying	wade
happiest	hiker	charging	chilly	cosy	wader
funnier	hiked	driest	chillier	cosier	waded
funniest	closing	surprising	chilliest	cosiest	wading
shinier	closer	scary	chilled	cosied	dive
shiniest	closed	crazy	chilling	cosying	diver
biking	tiniest	jolly	copy	make	dived
biker	amazing	late	copier	maker	diving
biked	changed	brave	copied	making	

1 Introduce/Review

- In preparation for the lesson, write up the following words, in pairs as shown, on the whiteboard:

  happier   *funnier*   *shinier*
  happiest   *funniest*   *shiniest*

- Read the words aloud to the children, then ask them to read them with you.
- Ask the children to identify the root word of each pair of words (*happy, funny, shiny*). Write the root word next to each pair of words.
- Involve individual children in underlining the suffix that has been added to each word (-*er*, -*est*).
- Challenge them to identify how the spelling of the root word changes when the suffix is added. (*The 'y' changes to an 'i'*.)
- Write this up as a spelling rule, e.g. 'When words end in 'y', the 'y' changes to an 'i' when the suffixes -*er* and -*est* are added.'
- Display this rule on the working wall, with the word list, and add to it as the unit progresses.
- Write up the following trios of words:

  biking   biker   biked   hiking   hiker   hiked   closing   closer   closed

- Repeat the process of reading the words aloud and involving the children in identifying the root words and suffixes.
- Challenge them to identify how the spelling of the root word changes when the suffix is added. (*The 'e' at the end of the word is dropped*.)
- Write this up as a spelling rule, e.g. 'When a word ends in 'e', the 'e' at the end of the word is dropped when the suffixes -*er*, -*ing* and -*ed* are added.'
- Display this rule, and the associated words, on the working wall, and refer to it regularly as the children go through the rest of the unit.
- If appropriate, write up other root words ending with an 'e' and explore what the word would look like if the final 'e' were not dropped when the suffix is added, e.g.

  make   makeer   late   lateest

- Explore how the words would be pronounced if the final 'e' were not dropped and establish that they are not words that exist in English.

Autumn term, Unit 1

Challenge!
Use the Spelling Fox Challenge: How does 'happy' become 'happier'? to kick off or consolidate the learning. The children must help the Spelling Fox find the correct answers! Access online via My Rising Stars.

2 Teach

- Give individual children A4 whiteboards with one focus root word written on each board, e.g. *chilly, copy, cosy, make, fade, dive*.
- Give other children the suffix cards (see You will need).
- Carry out a Living word activity by asking a child with a root word to stand at the front of the class. Ask the children with suffix cards to check whether their suffix could be added to the root word to make a real word. They can ask a friend if they are uncertain. They can then come out and add their suffix to the end of the root word. Involve the rest of the class in identifying and making the necessary changes in spelling. Once they are happy with the spelling of the word, write it on the whiteboard or on a large sheet of paper.
- Display the collections of words alongside the relevant spelling rule.

3 Practise

- Ask the children to work in pairs. Give each pair a copy of Ted, the Tiny Bear resource (see You will need), or display it on the whiteboard.
- Ask them to read it through and then reread it, identifying a suffix that could be added to each word in bold to make a new word that makes sense in the context of the passage. They can then write the correctly spelled new word in the space. (*Answers: tiniest, amazing, changed, fluffiest, charging, driest, surprising.*)
- Some children may need the support of a list of possible suffixes that could be added to the underlined words.
- Once they have completed the activity, ask each pair to join another pair and compare the spelling of the words they have added to the passage. Where there is a difference, they should check the spelling in a dictionary.
- The children can write the words that they have added to the passage in their word books or spelling journals.

4 Apply

- Write up the following root words: *scary, crazy, jolly, late, brave, cute* and the following suffixes: *-ed, -ing, -er* and *-est*.
- Ask the children to work independently and to choose up to three of the root words. They can then write down sentences that each use one of the root words plus one of the suffixes to make new words that are correctly spelled.
- Ask them to share their sentences with a friend and to check the spelling of the new words. If they are unsure of the correct spelling, they should check in a dictionary.

5 Review

- Re-visit and explore the spelling rules displayed on the working wall.
- Repeat the Living word activity from the Teach session, challenging the children with suffix cards to be the first to add their suffix to the root words. If appropriate, put a time limit on the activity.
- Ask two or three children with root words to stand at the front of the class and ask the rest of the children to experiment with adding the suffixes to work out which root word can take the most suffixes to produce real words, e.g.

    chilly – chillier, chilliest, chilled, chilling
    copy – copier, copied, copying
    cosy – cosier, cosiest, cosied, cosying
    make – maker, making
    fade – fader, faded, fading
    dive – diver, dived, diving

- If appropriate, draw attention to words that do not conform to the spelling rules identified earlier (*copying, cosying*). Write them up as if they did conform to the rule (*coping, cosing*) and encourage the children to read them aloud. Establish that either the meaning is different (*coping*) or the word does not exist (*cosing*).

© 2016 Rising Stars UK Ltd.

How does 'beauty' become 'beautiful'?

Focus: review of Year 2 suffixes (*-ness, -ment, -ful, -less*)

You will need:
Access online resources at My Rising Stars: www.risingstars-uk.com
- Root word cards per pair
- Suffix cards per pair
- Crossword per child
- Happy Pets resource per child

In a nutshell

Teacher subject knowledge for this unit:

This unit reviews year 2 work on suffixes, particularly when adding *-ness*, *-ment*, *-ful* and *-less*. If a word ends in 'y', the 'y' changes to 'i' when a suffix is added.

Word list

beauty	dull	friendly	hope	pay
bright	enjoy	happy	lonely	play
crazy	fear	heavy	move	sad

1 Introduce/Review

- In preparation for the lesson, write up the following root words in a column on the left-hand side of the whiteboard or large sheet of paper:

   happy   sad   friendly   lonely   bright   dull

- Write the following suffixes in a column down the right-hand side:

   -ful   -ness   -less   -ment

- Ask the children to work in pairs to identify which suffix can be added to all the root words to make a new word (*-ness*).
- Write up the new words, asking the children to help you to spell them. Establish that if a word ends in 'y', the 'y' changes to 'i' when the suffix is added.
- Write this up as a spelling rule: *If a word ends in 'y', the 'y' changes to 'i' when a suffix is added.* Display the rule alongside the root words and the 'new' words on the working wall.
- If appropriate, check their understanding of the words by asking them to produce sentences orally that each contain one of the words.

2 Teach

- On the whiteboard or on a large sheet of paper, write up the following words:

   playful   beautiful   craziness   heaviness   enjoyment

- Challenge the children to identify and correctly spell the root word in each word. Write up their responses, e.g. *play, beauty, crazy, heavy, enjoy*.
- Re-visit the spelling rule created earlier. Ask which words do not follow the rule (*play, enjoy*) and establish that the 'y' at the end of these words is part of the 'ay' or 'oy' spelling pattern rather than the /i/ sound spelled 'y'.
- Ask them to add the suffixes to the root words again and to spell the new words correctly. Write up the words as they say and spell them.
- Read the words aloud together, pronouncing them clearly.

3 Practise

- Give pairs of children sets of the root word cards and suffix cards (see You will need).
- Ask them to lay out the suffix cards in a row so that they work as headings. They can then arrange the word cards beneath the suffix that could be added to make a real word, e.g. the root word card *sad* goes beneath suffix *-ness*. Point out that some words are duplicated and can be put under more than one suffix, e.g. *fear* can go under *-ful* and *-less*.

Autumn term, Unit 2

Challenge!
Use the Spelling Fox Challenge: How does 'beauty' become 'beautiful'? to kick off or consolidate the learning. The children must help the Spelling Fox find the correct answers! Access online via My Rising Stars.

- Remind the children of the spelling rule generated earlier. Ask them to write the new words in their word books or spelling journals, checking the spelling carefully as they write.
- Display the correctly spelled words and ask the children to check each other's spelling.

    Answers:

fearful	*playful*	*loneliness*	*hopeless*
fearless	*payment*	*brightness*	*movement*
sadness	*happiness*	*hopeful*	*beautiful*

- Challenge them to spot the root words ending with a 'y' that do not change to an 'i' when a suffix is added, e.g. *play* and *pay*. Ask what they notice about the pronunciation of these words. *(The ending is pronounced /ai/.)* Ask them to say other words that end with a 'y', e.g. *happy, lonely*. What do they notice about the pronunciation? *(The ending is pronounced /i/.)* Establish that when words end with a 'y', pronounced /i/, the 'y' changes to an 'i'.

4 Apply

- Give a copy of the crossword (see You will need) to each child. If necessary, explain how to complete a crossword. Allow them time to read and work out the clues.
- Once they have finished, they can compare their completed crosswords with a partner to check that they have spelled the words correctly. If there are any discrepancies, suggest that they check the spelling of the word in a dictionary.
- Discuss the meanings of the words in the crossword and, if appropriate, how the suffixes help to work out word meanings, e.g. adding *-ness* to an adjective makes a noun that means *being or feeling a certain way*; adding *-ment* makes a noun from a verb and shows the result of the verb; adding *-ful* to a noun makes an adjective that means *full of*; adding *-less* to a verb makes an adjective meaning *without*.

    Answers:

    Across: 1. beautiful, 4. craziness, 5. joyful, 6. careless
    Down: 2. tidiness, 3. hurtful

5 Review

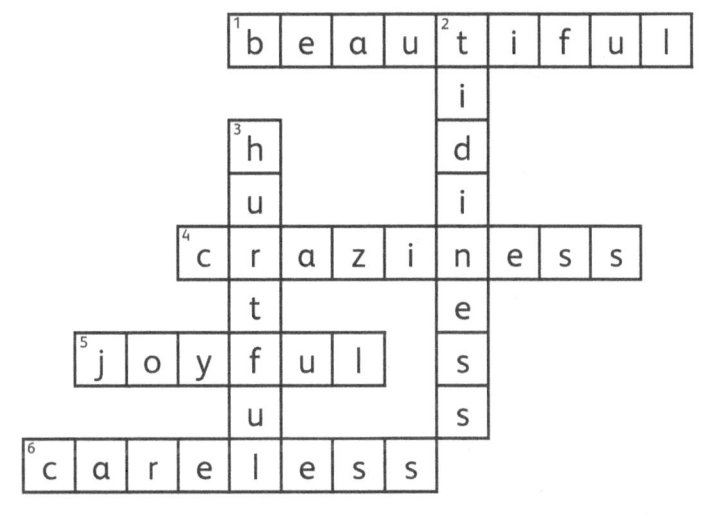

- Re-visit and discuss the spelling rule displayed on the working wall.
- Give each child a copy of the Happy Pets resource (see You will need), and read it to them, asking them to follow on their versions. When you reach a bold word, pronounce it clearly and give them time to write the word in the gap. In order to spell them correctly, the children need to be able to identify the root words so, if necessary, say what the root words are. You could also discuss the passage with the children and ask retrieval and inference questions.
- Once the children have completed the activity, give them time to check the spelling of the words they have added. They can then compare their spellings with those of a partner.

Can we spell words from our word list?

Focus: words from the Year 3/4 word list

You will need:
Access online resources at My Rising Stars: www.risingstars-uk.com
- Bean bags
- Focus word sentences for display
- Mind the gap resource per child
- Jack and Jill resource per child

In a nutshell

Teacher subject knowledge for this unit:

These 13 words are taken from the statutory word list for Year 3/4. In addition to the well-established 'look, say, cover, write, check' strategy, the children can use techniques that incorporate a range of learning styles, e.g. identifying the tricky bits of words, visualising the word and specific spelling patterns, pronouncing the words and clearly emphasising the syllables, chanting the spelling aloud, using actions and drawing images.

Word list						
accident	actual	address	answer	appear	arrive	believe
bicycle	breath	breathe	build	busy	business	

1 Introduce/Review

- In preparation for the lesson, write up the focus words: *accident, actual, address, answer, appear, arrive, believe, bicycle, breath, breathe, build, busy, business.*
- Read them aloud to the children, asking them to follow as you read, then to repeat each word after you. Pronounce them clearly and check their pronunciation.
- Read the words aloud a second time, asking them to read with you.
- Read each word once more, asking the children to listen carefully and then, as a class, identify the number of syllables in each word. Write the number of syllables next to each word on the list. Display this on the working wall and ask the children to write the words accurately in their word books or spelling journals.
- Involve the children in using each word in a sentence to demonstrate its meaning. Display the Focus word sentences (see You will need) and encourage the children to read them independently.

2 Teach

- Return to the list of focus words and look at the first four (*accident, actual, address, answer*). Read them aloud, pronouncing them clearly. Discuss which parts of the words might be tricky to spell, e.g. the double 'c' in *accident*, the silent 'w' in *answer*. Say the words, this time accentuating the individual letter sounds. Suggest to the children that saying the words like this might help them to remember how to spell the words correctly.
- Ask them to look carefully at the four words, to read the sentences containing the words and then to close their eyes and picture the words.
- Encourage the children to spell the words aloud to you without looking at them. Write up the words and ask the children to check whether they are spelled correctly.
- Repeat this with the rest of the focus words, grouping them into fours or fives. Once all of the words are written up correctly, read through the list, pronouncing them clearly, then reread them, accentuating the tricky parts of the words.

3 Practise

- Take the children into an open area outside the classroom.
- Ask them to work in pairs and give each pair a bean bag. Play Word tennis with the focus words: call out a focus word and ask each pair to spell it, letter by letter, passing the bean bag to each other as they say each letter.

Autumn term, Unit 3

Challenge!
Use the Spelling Fox Challenge: Can we spell words from our word list? (1) to kick off or consolidate the learning. The children must help the Spelling Fox find the correct answers! Access online via My Rising Stars.

4 Apply

- Give each child a copy of the Mind the gap activity (see You will need). Ask them to fill in the gaps in each word with the correct letters.
- Once they have completed the activity, they can compare their answers with those of a friend.
- Establish whether there are any particular words, or parts of words, that are proving problematic and re-visit these. Write them up and, as a class, read each word and spell it aloud. Repeat this, increasing the pace each time.

Answers:

a	c	c	i	d	e	n	t	
a	c	t	u	a	l	l	y	
a	d	d	r	e	s	s		
a	n	s	w	e	r			
a	p	p	e	a	r			
a	r	r	i	v	e			
b	e	l	i	e	v	e		
b	i	c	y	c	l	e		
b	r	e	a	t	h			
b	r	e	a	t	h	e		
b	u	i	l	d				
b	u	s	y					
b	u	s	i	n	e	s	s	

5 Review

- Split the class into five mixed-ability and mixed-gender spelling teams. Give each child a copy of the Jack and Jill resource (see You will need). Explain that you are going to read the passage aloud, with the missing words. They should each fill in the missing words, spelling them correctly.
- Once you have read the passage, give them up to five minutes to work with the rest of their team to check their spellings and to make any necessary corrections.
- Ask each team to swap their completed passages with another team. Read the passage again, spelling out the focus words and asking the children to mark the passages in front of them. Award one mark for each word spelled correctly, up to a maximum of 13. Add up each team's total and declare a winner.

How do we spell the /i/ sound in words?

Focus: the /i/ sound spelled with a 'y'

You will need:
Access online resources at My Rising Stars: www.risingstars-uk.com
- Focus word cards
- Word search
- Write the word resource per child

In a nutshell

Teacher subject knowledge for this unit:

This unit teaches the children about spelling the /i/ sound with a 'y' other than at the ends of words. In some words, the short /i/ sound in the middle of the word is spelled with a 'y'. In multisyllabic words, the /i/ sound spelled with a 'y' is in the first syllable.

Word list

| gym | myth | hymn | syrup | lyrics | symbol |
| crystal | typical | mystery | pyramid | syllable | |

1 Introduce/Review

- In front of the class, write up the following words on the whiteboard or on a large sheet of paper. Say the words clearly before you write them, then spell them as you write:

    gym   myth   hymn

- If appropriate, involve the children in spelling parts of the word by asking, for example, what letters make the /th/ sound in *myth*. Challenge them to spot the silent letter in *hymn* ('n').
- Use each word in a sentence to help the children to understand the meanings of the words, e.g.

    a) I go to a **gym** to keep fit.
    b) A **myth** is a story told by the Ancient Greeks.
    c) A **hymn** is a type of song that is sung in church.

- Draw a simple image next to each word to help children to remember the meaning, e.g. a book to represent *myth*, musical notes to represent *hymn*.
- Challenge the children to identify what the words have in common and what they think the focus spelling pattern might be. (*The /i/ sound in the middle of words is spelled with a 'y'*.)
- Identify and underline the letter that makes the /i/ sound in the words ('y').
- Repeat the activity with the following words:

    syrup   lyrics   symbol   crystal

- Say each word clearly to help children to hear the /i/ sound in each word, draw an image to help the children to remember the meaning and use the words in sentences to help them understand their meanings, e.g.

    a) **Syrup** is very sweet and we eat it on pancakes.
    b) The words of a song are called **lyrics**.
    c) A **symbol** is a sign or picture that is used instead of a letter or a word.
    d) A sugar **crystal** is a small grain of sugar.

- Display the list of words on the working wall and ask the children to read each word.
- Carry out a quick-fire 'look, say, cover, write, check' with each word.

2 Teach

- Re-visit the list of words on the working wall. Ask the children to read the words and then to spell them aloud.
- Read and write up the next group of words, spelling them as you write and involving the children in spelling certain parts of the words:

    typical   mystery   pyramid

- Ask individual children to underline the /i/ sound in each word.

Autumn term, Unit 4

Challenge!
Use the Spelling Fox Challenge: How do we spell the /i/ sound in words? to kick off or consolidate the learning. The children must help the Spelling Fox find the correct answers! Access online via My Rising Stars.

- Involve them in developing sentences that include each word and in creating an image to help them to remember the meanings. Add these words to the list on the working wall.
- Re-visit the list of words, read them and ask the children to remind you of the focus spelling pattern. *(The /i/ sound is spelled with a 'y'.)*
- Read the words, pronouncing them clearly. Involve the children in identifying the syllables in each word by clapping them out.
- Ask them what they notice about the position of the letter 'y' (and the /i/ sound) in the words. *(They are in the first syllable.)*
- Read the words together, emphasising the first syllable in each word.
- Spell the words together, emphasising the /i/ sound or letter 'y' in each word.
- Write up the word 'syllable'. Ask what the children notice about the word. *(The /i/ sound is made by the letter 'y'.)* Add the word 'syllable' to the display on the working wall.

3 Practise

- Ask the children to work with a partner. Give each pair a set of the focus word cards. Challenge them to carry out an open sort by thinking of a way of sorting the cards into groups. You may wish to give some children ideas for grouping the words, e.g. by syllables, by letter following the 'y', by number of letters, into alphabetical order.
- Following the sorting activity – which focuses attention on the words, letters and spelling patterns – ask the children to individually complete the word search (see You will need). You may wish to give some children access to the focus word cards, drawing attention to the fact that each word appears twice in the word search. Others may not need this support.
- Once they have completed the word search, ask the children to check their answers with a partner. How many words have they found? Discuss how they went about looking for the words, e.g. looking for the letter 'y' and then reading around that letter, looking for letter strings that appear in the focus words. Ask whether they found one technique more effective than another.

4 Apply

- Return to the focus word list on the working wall. Together, read through the words.
- Give each child a copy of the Write the word activity (see You will need).
- Ask them to look closely at each picture and then write the word in the spaces next to it. You may wish to give some children the initial letter of each word as extra support.
- Ask them to check each other's spellings and take feedback on how many correct answers the class got. Identify whether there are any particular words that are causing problems. Re-visit those words, carrying out a quick 'look, say, cover, write, check' with each one.

5 Review

- Refer the children to the display of words on the working wall and ask them to explain to you what the focus of the spelling has been in this unit. *(The /i/ sound spelled 'y'.)*
- Together, read through the words.
- Play Shannon's game with four or five of the focus words by writing up the initial letter of one of the words followed by the appropriate number of dashes to represent the missing letters, e.g. p _ _ _ _ _. You may wish to concentrate on those that the children found challenging to spell correctly.

How can we spell the /u/ sound in words?

Focus: the /u/ sound spelled 'ou'

You will need:
Access online resources at My Rising Stars: www.risingstars-uk.com
- Focus word cards
- 'ou' spellings sheet per child and for display

In a nutshell

Teacher subject knowledge for this unit:

The short vowel /u/ sound can be made in different ways: 'u' (as in *tuck*), 'oe' (as in *does*), 'o' (as in *love*), 'oo' (as in *flood*) and 'ou' (as in *touch*). The final spelling pattern is the focus for this unit.

Word list

touch	double	cousin	nourish
young	trouble	enough	courage
tough	couple	encourage	
rough	country	flourish	

1 Introduce/Review

- Write up the following words on the whiteboard:

    touch   *young*   *rough*   *double*

- Read each word aloud, pronouncing it clearly. Ask the children to read them with you.
- Ask what sounds they can hear in the words, then focus on the sound in the middle of each word (/u/).
- Challenge the children to tell you which letters make the /u/ sound in the words ('ou') and involve them in underlining the letters that make that sound.
- Check their understanding of the meanings of the words by asking them to orally produce sentences that include one of the words.
- Display the sentences, with the focus words underlined, on the working wall.

2 Teach

- Play Shannon's game by writing up the initial letter of one of the words followed by the appropriate number of dashes to represent the missing letters, e.g. t _ _ _ _.
- Ask the children to suggest which letters could come next, writing in the correct letters until the word is complete.
- Read the word aloud, asking them to read it with you.
- Challenge them to identify the letters that make the /u/ sound.
- Repeat this with other words containing the 'ou' spelling pattern that they have not yet been introduced to, e.g. *tough, trouble, couple*.
- Display the completed words on the working wall.

3 Practise

- Give pairs of children the Focus word cards (see You will need). Ask them to sort the cards into two groups: words with the /u/ sound made with the 'ou' spelling pattern and words with the /u/ sound made by other letters. You may wish to challenge some children by asking them to do an open sort activity in which they choose their own categories.
- Once the children have completed their word sort, they can join with another pair to compare the groups they have produced.
- Take feedback from the sorting activity and display the grouped words on the working wall. Encourage the children to read through the words with you.

Autumn term, Unit 5

Challenge!

Use the Spelling Fox Challenge: How can we spell the /u/ sound in words? to kick off or consolidate the learning. The children must help the Spelling Fox find the correct answers! Access online via My Rising Stars.

4 Apply

- Display the following sentences on the whiteboard, or hand out individual copies (see You will need).
   a) I knew I was in t _ _ _ _ _ _ when I saw the broken window.
   b) I have two c _ _ _ _ _ _ who live in the c _ _ _ _ _ _.
   c) My brother is y _ _ _ _ _ _ than me.
   d) Mum said, 'Don't t _ _ _ _ _ _ the plate because it is very hot.'
   e) If someone is brave, it means they have c _ _ _ _ _ _.

  Answers: a) trouble, b) cousins; country, c) younger, d) touch, e) courage

- Challenge the children to write down the sentences and to fill the gap with a word containing the 'ou' spelling pattern making the /u/ sound. You may wish to give some children a selection of words to choose from. Others may not need the support of the initial letters of each word.
- Ask the children to check the spelling of the words they have written against the words displayed on the working wall. Take feedback. Are there any particular words that are causing problems?

5 Review

- Make sure that all children can see the words displayed on the working wall.
- Together, read through the collection of words containing the 'ou' spelling pattern. Check that the children are pronouncing them accurately.
- Play Speedy spelling by asking the children to stand behind their chairs. Say a word containing the /u/ sound formed by the 'ou' spelling pattern. Start with one child who says the first letter in the word, the next child should say the next letter in the word, and so on, until the word has been spelled. If a mistake is made, ask the child to sit down. Once the word is spelled, the children who remain standing call out 'Speedy spelling!' and sit down. You may wish to have a time limit in which the children have to spell each word.

Can you correct your own writing?

Focus: words from children's own writing

You will need:
Access online resources at My Rising Stars: www.risingstars-uk.com
- Word books or spelling journals
- Dictionaries

In a nutshell

Teacher subject knowledge for this unit:

Following discussion on strategies for remembering how to spell specific words, the 'look, say, cover, write, check' approach is used to practise and reinforce spellings. The focus words are re-visited a number of times through various approaches, giving children the opportunity to read and reread the words, as well as writing them down and using them in sentences.

> **Word list**
> Identified by the children from their own writing.

1 Introduce/Review

- Ask the children to look through any writing they have done in English, and in other subjects, and to find up to ten words that they have spelled incorrectly. These may well be words that have already been identified by you during marking. Some children might need adult support in identifying these words.
- Ask them to draw up a 'look, say, cover, write, check' table in their word books or spelling journals and to write their focus words in the left-hand column. They should then check that they have spelled them correctly by asking a friend, an adult, reading the marking comments or checking in a dictionary.
- Ask them to work in pairs and to read their lists to each other, discussing what the words mean and which parts of the words they find particularly tricky to spell.

2 Teach

- As a class, discuss techniques that the children can use to remember spellings, e.g. pronouncing all of the letters in a word, including those that are silent; visualising whole words and letter patterns; spotting words within words; breaking words down into root words and prefixes/suffixes.
- Ask them to carry out the 'look, say, cover, write, check' process with each of the words on their lists, completing the table in their word books or spelling journals. You may wish to put a time limit on the activity to focus their attention on the task.
- Once they have completed their 'look, say, cover, write, check' tables, they can check with a partner that they have spelled the words accurately. If there is any dispute, they can check in a dictionary.

3 Practise

- Ask the children to re-present their original word lists as two separate columns: those they *did* spell correctly after the 'look, say, cover, write, check' approach, and those they *did not*. They could use a tick or a cross as the heading for the relevant list.
- Put the children into pairs, ensuring that between them they have some incorrectly spelled words. Challenge them to teach each other to spell the words on the incorrectly spelled list, using some of the strategies that they explored earlier in this unit.

Autumn term, Unit 6

Challenge!
Use the Spelling Fox Challenge: Can you correct your own writing? (1) to kick off or consolidate the learning. The children must help the Spelling Fox find the correct answers! Access online via My Rising Stars.

4 Apply

- Ask the children to continue to work with their partners and to each choose five words from their original lists. They can then combine their words so that each pair has a collection of ten focus words.
- Challenge them to work together and to read and write the list of words with the aim of reducing the number of incorrectly spelled words every time they go through the list. Some children might benefit from a time limit on the activity.
- At the end of the session, ask how many incorrectly spelled words each pair of children have left on their lists.

5 Review

- Ask the children to return to their own individual spelling lists created at the beginning of this unit and to swap them with a partner.
- They should read out each word on their partner's list, giving their partner time to write the words down correctly but maintaining a steady pace.
- Once each child has had the opportunity to write down their words correctly, they should check each other's lists.
- Ask them to develop and write sentences that include their focus words to show that they understand the meanings of the words.

How can we spell the /ai/ sound?

Focus: the /ai/ sound spelled 'ei', 'eigh' or 'ey'

You will need:
Access online resources at My Rising Stars: www.risingstars-uk.com
- Focus word cards
- Write the word resource, per child
- Mind the gap resource, per child

In a nutshell

Teacher subject knowledge for this unit:

The /ai/ sound can be spelled in a variety of ways: 'ai' (*rain*), 'ay' (*day*), 'ea' (*great*), 'a_e' (*brave*), 'a' (*baby*), 'ei' (*beige*), 'ey' (*grey*) and 'eigh' (*weight*). The focus spelling patterns for this unit are 'ei', 'eigh' and 'ey'.

Word list				
they	grey	obey	beige	sleigh
neigh	neighbour	eight	eighth	weight
reins	reign	vein	veil	height

1 Introduce/Review

- Before the start of this unit, write up the following focus words on the whiteboard or on a large sheet of paper:

  they   grey   obey   beige   sleigh   neigh   neighbour   eight
  eighth   weight   reins   reign   vein   veil   height

- Read the words aloud to the children, pronouncing them clearly. Then ask them to read the words with you, and finally to read them independently.
- Ask the children what they notice about the words and challenge them to work out what the focus spelling pattern might be in this unit. (*The /ai/ sound spelled 'ei', 'eigh' or 'ey'.*)
- Ask them to work with a partner and to read the words to each other. Are they able to hear one word that does not sound the same as the others? (*height*)
- Involve individual children in underlining the letters in each word that make the /ai/ sound.
- Check that they can all say the /ai/ sound clearly and ensure that they are aware of the focus spelling patterns that make that sound.
- Display the focus words on the working wall.

2 Teach

- Re-visit the focus words displayed on the working wall. Encourage the children to read them aloud with you, emphasising the /ai/ sound in each word.
- Challenge them to create an oral /ai/ rhyming string around the class. You may wish to start them off by giving a word that contains the /ai/ sound, reminding them that the words they produce can be nonsense words but must contain the /ai/ *sound* but not necessarily a focus spelling pattern, e.g. *may, bay, rain, main, lein, tein*. The idea is to emphasise the /ai/ sound orally.
- Play Shannon's game by writing up the initial letter of one of the focus words followed by the appropriate number of dashes to represent the missing letters, e.g. s _ _ _ _ _.
- Ask the children to suggest which letters could come next, writing in the correct letters until the word is complete.
- Read the word aloud, asking them to read it with you.
- Challenge them to identify the letters that make the /ai/ sound.
- Repeat this with other words containing the 'ei', 'eigh' or 'ey' spelling pattern, e.g. *grey, weight, rein*.
- Display the completed words on the working wall.

3 Practise

- Return to the focus list of words. Ask the children to talk to a partner and share ideas about how they could sort or group the words. Take feedback from the discussion, encouraging

Autumn term, Unit 7

Challenge!
Use the Spelling Fox Challenge: How can we spell the /ai/ sound? to kick off or consolidate the learning. The children must help the Spelling Fox find the correct answers! Access online via My Rising Stars.

the children to support their ideas with reasons. They might suggest grouping the words by number of syllables, organising them alphabetically or sorting by spelling pattern. Explore which of these might help them to remember the spelling of the words.
- Give pairs of children sets of the focus word cards.
- Ask them to read the words carefully, saying them aloud, and then sort them into groups according to the spelling of the /ai/ sound.
- The children can then write the words, in their groups, in their word books or spelling journals.
- Set the children a number of challenges, e.g. identify a word with a silent letter (*reign*), a two-syllable word (*obey* or *neighbour*), two words that are colours (*grey*, *beige*), two pairs of words where only one letter is different (*veil* and *vein*, *rein* and *reign*), two words that are homophones (*rein* and *reign*).
- Ask each pair of children to join up with another pair to set each other similar challenges that involve close reading of the words and the spelling of the words, as well as listening carefully.

4 Apply

- Re-visit the grouping of the words according to the spelling pattern. Ask the children to identify how many different ways the /ai/ sound can be spelled, according to the word list. (Three: 'ei', 'eigh' and 'ey'.)
- Give each child a copy of the Write the word resource (see You will need) and ask them to complete the sheet.
- Once they have finished, they can either check each other's spellings or you may wish to mark it in order to get an idea of any particular words that the children are finding problematic.
- Re-visit those words with groups of children, or the whole class, using a variety of spelling strategies to reinforce the spelling.

5 Review

- Give each child a copy of the Mind the gap activity (see You will need). Explain that they should fill in the missing letters in each word in order to spell them correctly. Once they have filled in all of the missing letters, and if they have spelled each word correctly, the letters in the shaded boxes will spell one of the focus words.
- You may wish to give some children the focus word cards to support them as they complete the activity.
- Allow the children time to complete the activity. Ask what word they have produced.
- Give them time to check each other's spellings.

    Answers:

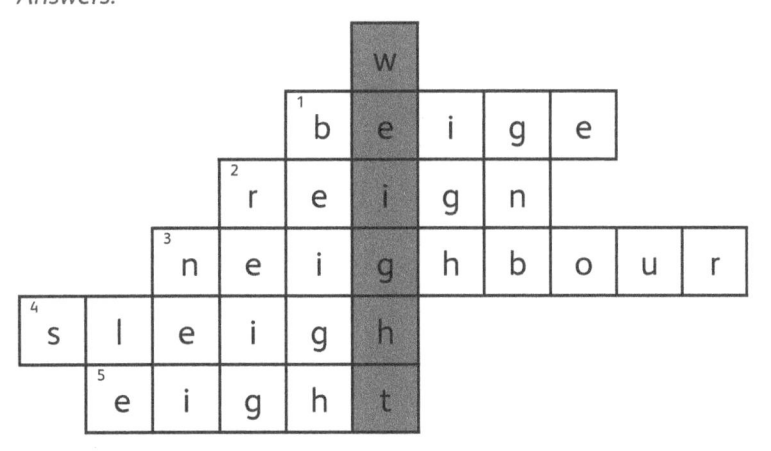

				w				
		1	b	e	i	g	e	
		2	r	e	i	g	n	
	3	n	e	i	g	h	b	o	u	r
4	s	l	e	i	g	h		
	5	e	i	g	h	t		

© 2016 Rising Stars UK Ltd.

How can we use prefixes?

Focus: the *un-*, *dis-* and *mis-* prefixes

You will need:
Access online resources at My Rising Stars: www.risingstars-uk.com
- Poor Frog! resource per pair
- Focus word cards
- Unhappy Frog! resource, per child
- A4 whiteboards and pens

In a nutshell

Teacher subject knowledge for this unit:

Prefixes are groups of letters that can be put at the beginning of root words and often change the meaning of the word. The prefixes *un-*, *dis-* and *mis-* turn words into negatives. These prefixes all mean *not*.

Word list

happy	like	behave	appear	able	lucky	well
understand	spell	honest	agree	likely	fasten	place
fortunate	wanted	comfort	fortune	loved		

1 Introduce/Review

- Challenge the class to tell you what a prefix is. Can they give an example of a prefix?
- Write up these words on the whiteboard:

    happy   like   behave

- Read them aloud, pronouncing them clearly, and ask the children to read them with you. Discuss their understanding of the meanings of the words. Encourage the children to use each word in a sentence to show that they understand the meaning. If necessary, demonstrate how to do this, e.g. *Kayleigh is happy when she is playing with her best friend.*
- Write up some of the sentences that the children produce.
- Challenge the children to turn the word *happy* into a word with the opposite meaning by adding a prefix. You may wish to give them the prefix (*un-*) or leave it up to them to work out.
- Add the prefix *un-* to the word *happy* in the written sentence and ask them whether they would like to change anything else in the sentence to help with the meaning of the word *unhappy*, e.g. adding the word *not* before *playing*.
- Establish that *happy* and *unhappy* have the opposite meaning.
- Repeat this activity with the other two words: *like* (*dislike*), *behave* (*misbehave*). Establish that adding the prefixes *un-*, *dis-* and *mis-* turn positive words into negative words.
- Summarise this as a sentence and display it, along with some examples of words, on the working wall.
- Give pairs of children the Poor Frog! resource (see You will need). Read it aloud, emphasising the incorrect words, and ask them what is wrong with what Frog is saying.
- Challenge the children to work together to put Frog right and to correct his incorrect words, writing them in the spaces.
- Read the passage aloud, now using the correct words. Take feedback to get an idea of which words are familiar to the children.

2 Teach

- Draw up a smiley face and a sad face. Underneath the smiley face, write four or five words that can take one of the focus prefixes (*un-*, *dis-*, *mis-*), e.g. *appear, able, lucky, well*. Ask the children to turn the positive words into negative words by adding the correct prefix. Establish that the focus prefixes all have negative meanings and that they can be used to create words with the opposite meaning of the original. Also establish that the spelling of a root word does not change when these prefixes are added.

Autumn term, Unit 8

Challenge!
Use the Spelling Fox Challenge: How can we use prefixes? (1) to kick off or consolidate the learning. The children must help the Spelling Fox find the correct answers! Access online via My Rising Stars.

- Give pairs of children A4 whiteboards. Using the focus word cards (see You will need), hold up one word at a time and challenge them to write an appropriate prefix on their whiteboards and to hold it up so that you can see it. Use this as an opportunity to quickly assess which children are suggesting correct prefixes and which are unable to do so. You may wish to provide extra support to those who are suggesting incorrect, or no, prefixes.

3 Practise

- Ask the children to work in pairs. Give each pair a set of the focus word cards. On separate sheets of paper or A4 whiteboards, ask them to write the three focus prefixes. Using these as headings, they can then sort the focus word cards into groups under an appropriate heading.
- Once they are happy with their groupings, ask them to choose between three and five words and to orally rehearse sentences that include the words used accurately.
- Once they have agreed on the sentences, they can write them down in their word books or spelling journals.
- Take feedback from the activity, discuss some of the sentences and whether they make sense. Transfer some sentences that use the focus prefixes accurately to the working wall.
- Read the sentences together and discuss the meanings of the focus words. As a class, chant the spelling of the focus words together, letter by letter.

4 Apply

- Give each child a copy of the reading passage, Unhappy Frog! (see You will need). Explain that they should choose prefixes that they think fit the bold words to make a new word that makes sense in the passage.
- Ask the children to share their completed reading passages and to explore any examples where they have added different prefixes to the words. Take feedback from the activity, asking the children to call out the words that they have used in the passage. Write up a list of the correct words and ask the children to double check and correct their own passages.
- They can then write the list of words, correctly spelled, in their word books or spelling journals.

5 Review

- Give six individual children A4 whiteboards and pens and ask them to each write one of the following words on their board:

    understand   spell   honest   agree   likely   fasten

- Give a further three children A4 whiteboards and ask them each to write one of the following prefixes on their whiteboards:

    un-   dis-   mis-

- Carry out a Living word activity by asking the children with the root words to stand at the front of the class and ask the rest of the class to support the children with the prefixes in creating proper words by adding themselves to the beginning of the root words.
- Challenge the children to create sentences orally that include one or more of the new words.

When do we double the consonant?
Focus: adding suffixes

You will need:
Access online resources at My Rising Stars: www.risingstars-uk.com
- Word family cards
- Missing words resource per child
- Naughty Miss Muffet resource, per child
- Dictionaries

In a nutshell
Teacher subject knowledge for this unit:

In a word where two vowels are separated by a consonant (a split digraph), the first vowel is usually long (*hope*). A double consonant means the first vowel is short (*hopped*). So, when you add an ending to a short vowel word, you double the consonant (e.g. *run + -ing = running, sun + -y = sunny*). The spelling rule is: *When you add a suffix that starts with a vowel to a short vowel word, you usually double the consonant.*

Word list

run	runner	running	runny	begin	beginner	beginning	
sun	sunny	sunnier	sunniest	prefer	preferred	preferring	
hot	hotter	hottest		admit	admitting	admitted	admittance
fat	fatter	fatten	fatty	fattiest	equip	equipped	equipping
pat	patter	patting	patty	occur	occurring	occurred	occurrence
drop	dropper	dropping		regret	regretted	regretting	
sad	sadder	sadden	saddest	forbid	forbidden	forbidding	

1 Introduce/Review

- Write up the following words on the whiteboard:

    bet   dine   hope   run

- Encourage the children to read them aloud with you. Ask them to look closely at the words and to tell you something about them, e.g. they all have one syllable, two have long vowel sounds (*hope, dine*), two have short vowel sounds (*bet, run*).
- Ask the children to work with a partner. Give them a limited amount of time, e.g. two minutes, to write down as many words as they can that contain the four focus words, e.g. *hopping, hopper, hopped, hops, hoped, hopes, hoping, diner, dined, dines, dinner.*
- Write up the four original focus words as headings. Take feedback from the activity, recording the words the children give you under the relevant heading. Add to the lists yourself where necessary. Focus on one of the word lists and read the words aloud.
- Ask the children to spend a short time discussing with a partner anything they notice about the words in the list, e.g. number of syllables, spelling patterns, long/short vowel sounds. Discuss their observations.

2 Teach

- Return to the word lists created in the previous session. Focus on one and ask the children to suggest ways that the words could be grouped or sorted. Guide them towards grouping the words containing double consonants together, then add words with double consonants from the other word lists.
- Challenge them to work out why some of the words contain double consonants and others do not. Together, establish that where two vowels are separated by a consonant, the first vowel is usually long (*hope*). A double consonant means the first vowel is short (*hopped*). So, when you add an ending to a short vowel word, you double the consonant (*run + -ing = running, sun + -y = sunny*). Write this up as the focus spelling rule, e.g. 'When you add a suffix that starts with a vowel to a short vowel word, you usually double the consonant.' Display the spelling rule on the working wall, along with examples of words that illustrate it.

Autumn term, Unit 9

Challenge!
Use the Spelling Fox Challenge: When do we double the consonant? to kick off or consolidate the learning. The children must help the Spelling Fox find the correct answers! Access online via My Rising Stars.

- Re-visit the word lists and read the words containing double consonants aloud, emphasising the short vowel sound as you read. Check that the children are able to differentiate between short and long vowel sounds.
- Introduce words with more than one syllable that end in a single consonant, e.g. *begin, admit, equip, occur, regret, forbid*. As a class, experiment with adding suffixes that start with a vowel to check whether the focus spelling rule still applies, e.g. *beginner, beginning; admitted, admittance, admitting*.

3 Practise

- You will need an open space where the children can move around freely. Before the activity, choose families of words from the Word family cards (see You will need) that are suitable for the children in terms of reading and understanding.
- Give each child in the class a Word family card, telling them not to show it to anyone else. Explain that the word on their card belongs to a word family and their job is to find the rest of their family. They should read their card, say the word aloud to themselves and then move around the space repeating their word and listening out for other words that could be part of their family. Once they find another member of their word family, they continue to move around together. Remind them not to show their card to anyone.
- You can either put a time limit on this activity or wait until all of the children have found their word families.
- Discuss what they had to do to find the rest of their family, and what they found helpful, e.g. pronouncing their word clearly, listening carefully.
- Ask each word family to sit together and to lay out their cards so that they can all see them. Ask each group to sort their cards into words with double consonants and words with single consonants. Ask whether their words with double consonants follow the spelling rule.

4 Apply

- Give each child a copy of the Missing words activity (see You will need). Ask them to read each sentence carefully and to turn the root word into a longer word by adding a suffix beginning with a vowel. Remind them of the spelling focus for this unit and that the final consonant of the root word will need to be doubled.
- Once the children have completed the sheet, they can work with a partner to compare the spellings of their new words. If they have written something different, they should decide which spelling is correct and change it or check the spelling in a dictionary.
- They can then record the root word and new words in their word books or spelling journals.

5 Review

- Re-visit the focus spelling rule displayed on the working wall: 'When you add a suffix that starts with a vowel to a short vowel word, you usually double the consonant.'
- Remind the children of how it works by looking at the word lists created during this unit.
- Give each child a copy of the Naughty Miss Muffet resource (see You will need). Read the passage aloud to the children, allowing them time to write in the missing words. Give them the hint that the missing words all follow the focus spelling rule.
- Once the activity is completed, ask the children to work with a partner to check the spelling of the words they have added to the passage. If there is any difference of opinion, they can check it against the word lists on the working wall or in a dictionary.

How can we spell long vowel sounds?
Focus: spelling split digraphs

You will need:
Access online resources at My Rising Stars: www.risingstars-uk.com
- A4 whiteboards and pens
- The Lost Sheep resource per child
- Loop game cards

In a nutshell
Teacher subject knowledge for this unit:

This unit covers how to spell long vowel sounds when two vowel sounds are split by a consonant. A split digraph means two letters making one sound that is split by another letter, e.g. *cake* – the /ai/ sound is made from 'a_e' split by 'k'. This is often referred to as the magic 'e'.

Word list				
arrive	cake	complete	decide	describe
extreme	guide	home	surprise	time

1 Introduce/Review

- Write up the following words:

    tap   rip   hop   cub

- Ask the children to talk to a partner about one letter that could be added to the end of each of the words to create a new word. Take feedback and add their suggested letters to the end of the words. Establish that 's' can be added in order to produce plurals, but focus on adding 'e', which produces a new word in each case, e.g. *tape, ripe, hope, cube*. Check the children's understanding of the new words by encouraging them to use the words in sentences.
- Introduce or re-visit the term 'split digraph', meaning two letters making one sound that is split by another letter. In the word list, identify the digraph in each case and the letter that is splitting that digraph, e.g. in *tape*, the digraph is 'ae', the letter splitting that digraph is 'p'.
- Write up a definition of a split digraph and display it on the working wall, along with words as examples.
- Write up the following words:

    hoe   tie   cue

- Read them aloud and then demonstrate how to add in a letter to create new words with a split digraph, e.g. *home, tire, cute*.
- Write up other words, e.g. *toe, doe, die, lie*, and challenge the children to add in a letter to make a new word with a split digraph, e.g. *tone, tore, dome, lice, lime*.
- Establish that in a split digraph, the vowel sound made is like in the letter's 'name'.

2 Teach

- Explain to the children that they are going to be looking at longer words with split digraphs.
- Write up the following words:

    arrive   decide   describe   extreme   exercise   guide

- Read them aloud to the children, emphasising the part of the word with the split digraph, e.g. *arrive*, *decide*. Ask them to read the words aloud with you, again emphasising the split digraph. Involve some children in underlining or highlighting the split digraph in the words.
- Give pairs of children an A4 whiteboard and pen each. Explain that you are going to say a sound that is spelled with a split digraph and they should listen carefully and then write down the letters that they think spell the sound. Say /ive/ (as in *hive*) clearly and give the children time to write down the letters that they think spell that sound. Ask them to hold up their whiteboards so that you can check what they have written in order to make sure

Autumn term, Unit 10

> **Challenge!**
> Use the Spelling Fox Challenge: How can we spell long vowel sounds? to kick off or consolidate the learning. The children must help the Spelling Fox find the correct answers! Access online via My Rising Stars.

that they understand the activity. Repeat this with other sounds, e.g. /ide/, /ibe/, /eme/, /ise/, /ide/, asking them to write down the letters that spell the sound and to hold up their whiteboards. If you identify that the children are finding a particular digraph challenging, repeat the sound a number of times, checking what they have written each time.
- End by re-visiting the spelling focus and ask them to explain it to you, giving examples of words that contain split digraphs. Challenge them to produce words of more than one syllable, e.g. *surprise*.

3 Practise

- Split the class into five or six teams, each containing around five children. Explain that each team will be given a word. Their challenge is to write down as many words as they can that rhyme with their word. Remind them to think about words with more than one syllable – it is the final sound that is important – but emphasise that the words they write down must be real words.
- Give out one of the following words to each group: *late, rice, tide, mile, hive, rope*, and set a time limit for the activity. If necessary, support some of the groups as they compile their lists.
- Take feedback from the activity. If groups have recorded words that rhyme but have incorrect spellings (e.g. *sope*), challenge them to think about the correct spelling. Write up the incorrect word, then write it correctly and put a large cross through the incorrectly spelled word. Alternatively, you may wish to create a 'trash' box and, with a sense of drama, throw any incorrect words into the box.

4 Apply

- Give children copies of The Lost Sheep resource (see You will need).
- Read the passage aloud and ask them to fill in the missing words. Remind them of the spelling focus and that the words will end with a split digraph.
- Once they have completed the passage, give them some time to read through and check their words.
- Encourage the children to compare their passages with a partner, checking the spelling of words where necessary.

5 Review

- Explain to the children that they are going to play a Loop game (see You will need) that focuses on split digraphs. If necessary, explain how this works and demonstrate with the first couple of questions and answers.
- Ask the children to work in pairs. Give out a card to each pair of children. Start the game by choosing a pair to read the definition at the bottom. The pair with the correct linked word at the top of their card should read it out and then read the definition at the bottom of their card.
- Once the game is complete, repeat it two or three times, challenging the children to speed up each time.

Can we spell words from our word list?

Focus: words from the Year 3/4 word list

You will need:
Access online resources at My Rising Stars: www.risingstars-uk.com
- A4 whiteboards and pens
- Mind the gap resource per child
- The race of the century resource per child

In a nutshell

Teacher subject knowledge for this unit:

These nine words are taken from the word list for Year 3/4. They all start with the letter 'c'. In some cases, this is pronounced as a soft 'c' (*centre*). In others, it is pronounced as a hard 'c' (*calendar*). A hard 'c' is followed by 'a' or 'o'. A soft 'c' is followed by an 'e' or 'i'.

In addition to the well-established 'look, say, cover, write, check' strategy, the children can use techniques that incorporate a range of learning styles, e.g. identifying the tricky bits of words, visualising the word and specific spelling patterns, pronouncing the words clearly and emphasising the syllables, chanting the spelling aloud, using actions and drawing images.

Word list

calendar	caught	centre	century	certain
circle	complete	consider	continue	

1 Introduce/Review

- In preparation for this lesson, write up the following words:

calendar	caught	centre	century	certain
circle	complete	consider	continue	

- Read the words aloud to the children, pronouncing them clearly. Ask them to read the words aloud with you. Monitor their pronunciation of the words.
- Ask them to work with a partner to produce a sentence that includes one or more of the words. Take feedback and set a challenge by asking *Who can use the most focus words in one sentence?* E.g. 'My eye was **caught** by a large **circle** in the **centre** of the 21st-**century calendar**.'
- Reread the list of words and discuss which parts of the words the children think are particularly tricky to spell.
- Write two or three of the words, underlining the tricky bit, e.g. *calenda̲r̲*, *c̲aught̲*, *cent̲re̲*.
- Ask the children to write down the words, checking that they are spelled correctly, in their word books or spelling journals and to underline the parts of the words that they find particularly tricky.

2 Teach

- Return to the list of the focus words. Ask the children, in pairs, to think about how many different ways they could sort the words into groups, e.g. number of syllables, alphabetically by second letter, by initial sound.
- Lead them to deciding to group the words according to the initial sound. Give nine children A4 whiteboards and ask them to each write one of the focus words on their whiteboards and to stand at the front of the class. Involve the rest of the class in grouping the children according to the initial sound of the words that they are holding (*calendar, caught; centre, century, certain; circle; complete, consider, continue*).
- Ask what the class notice about the second letter in each word. (*They are vowels.*)
- Give other children in the class A4 whiteboards and ask them to work with a partner to note down other words that could be added to the four groups at the front of the class, e.g. *card, cell, citrus, comic*.
- Ask what they notice about the initial sound of the letter 'c' in each group. (*A hard 'c' is followed by an 'a' or 'o'. A soft 'c' is followed by an 'e' or 'i'.*) Summarise this discovery as a sentence and display it on the working wall.

Autumn term, Unit 11

Challenge!
Use the Spelling Fox Challenge: Can we spell words from our word list? (2) to kick off or consolidate the learning. The children must help the Spelling Fox find the correct answers! Access online via My Rising Stars.

- Are they able to suggest any consonants that could follow the letter 'c' at the beginning of a word? ('h' – as in children, 'l' – as in clown, 'r' – as in crown, 'y' – as in cyber.) If appropriate, draw attention to the soft 'c' when followed by 'y' – the 'y' sounds like an 'i'.

3 Practise

- Ask the children to revisit their list of focus words in their word books or spelling journals.
- Ask them to work with a partner and to carry out a Guess my word activity. One child chooses a word from the list of focus words and gives their partner clues about the word, e.g. 'It starts with a soft 'c', it's a noun.' The child guessing the word starts with five points and loses a point each time they cannot guess the word or make an incorrect guess. Once the 'guesser' has worked out the word, they should write it down and ask their partner to check the spelling. Ask the pairs to keep individual scores and check which child in the class has the highest (and winning) score.
- Come back together as a class and discuss whether there are any words remaining that the children are still finding challenging. Spell the words aloud together, writing them up so that all of the children can see them.

4 Apply

- Give each child a copy of the Mind the gap activity (see You will need). Ask them to look at the clues and to fill in the missing letters in each word. The letters in the shaded boxes will make one of the focus words.
- Once they have completed their grid, they should compare it with a friend's. Where they have used different letters, they should check against the original word list in their word books or spelling journals and make any necessary changes.
- As a class, spell the words aloud together and write them up as you do so.

    Answers:

    1. caught
    2. complete
    3. central
    4. centre
    5. certain
    6. circle

5 Review

- Give each child a copy of The race of the century (see You will need). Read the passage aloud to the children, giving them time to think about and write in each missing word.
- Once they have completed the passage, give them time to read and check the spelling of the words before they compare it with a partner. They can check any words that they are unsure of in a dictionary.

    The race of the century

    I was **certain** that I was being followed as I ran through the **centre** of the forest. I stopped to **consider** what I should do and decided to **continue** on my way. After a while I was convinced that I had run in a **complete circle** and that I would soon be **caught**. I must not fail. This was the race of the **century**. The one that had been on my **calendar** for months.

Can you correct your own writing?

Focus: words from children's own writing

You will need:
Access online resources at My Rising Stars: www.risingstars-uk.com
- Dictionaries
- Word books or spelling journals
- Bean bags

In a nutshell

Teacher subject knowledge for this unit:

This unit focuses on words that the children identify as incorrectly spelled in their own writing.

Following discussion on strategies for remembering how to spell specific words, the 'look, say, cover, write, check' approach is used to practise and reinforce spellings. The focus words are re-visited a number of times through various activities, giving children the opportunity to read and reread the words, as well as writing them down and using them in sentences.

> **Word list**
>
> Identified by the children from their own writing.

1 Introduce/Review

- Ask the children to look through any writing they have done in English, and in other subjects, and to find up to ten words that they have spelled incorrectly. These may well be words that have already been identified by you during marking. Some children might need adult support in identifying these words.
- Ask them to draw up a 'look, say, cover, write, check' table in their word books or spelling journals and to write the target words in the left-hand column. They should then check that they have spelled them correctly by asking a friend, an adult, checking the marking comments or checking in a dictionary.
- Ask them to work in pairs and to read their lists to each other, discussing what the words mean and which parts of the words they find particularly tricky to spell.

2 Teach

- As a class, discuss techniques that the children can use to remember spellings, e.g. pronouncing all letters in a word, including those that are silent; visualising whole words and letter patterns; spotting words within words; breaking words down into root words and prefixes/suffixes.
- Ask them to carry out the 'look, say, cover, write, check' process with each of the words on their lists, completing the table in their word books or spelling journals. You may wish to put a time limit on the activity to focus the children's attention on the task.
- Once they have completed their 'look, say, cover, write, check' tables, they can check with a partner that they have spelled the words accurately.

3 Practise

- Ask the children to re-present their original word lists as two separate columns: those they *did* spell correctly after the 'look, say, cover, write, check' approach, and those they *did not*. They could use a tick or a cross as the heading for the relevant list.
- Ask the children to work in pairs and give each pair a bean bag. Ask them to choose a word from their incorrectly spelled list, to both read it and then to play Word tennis, spelling the word letter by letter, passing the bean bag to each other as they say each letter. They can repeat this with other words from their lists.

Autumn term, Unit 12

Challenge!
Use the Spelling Fox Challenge: Can you correct your own writing? (2) to kick off or consolidate the learning. The children must help the Spelling Fox find the correct answers! Access online via My Rising Stars.

4 Apply

- Ask the children to continue to work with their partners and to each choose five words from their original lists. They can then combine their words so that each pair has a collection of ten focus words.
- Challenge them to choose at least five words from their collection and to produce sentences that contain those five words. They can write out those sentences, leaving gaps for the focus words. They can then join up with another pair and swap their missing words sentences, reading them aloud to each other and writing in the missing words. They can then check each other's spelling of the missing words.

5 Review

- Ask the children to return to their own individual spelling lists created at the beginning of this unit and to swap them with a partner.
- They should read out each word on their partner's list, giving their partner time to write the words down correctly but maintaining a steady pace.
- Once each child has had the opportunity to write down their words correctly, they should check each other's lists.
- Ask them to develop and write sentences that include their focus words to show that they understand the meanings of the words.

Who will win the spelling quiz?
Focus: review of Autumn term spellings

You will need:
Access online resources at My Rising Stars: www.risingstars-uk.com
- A4 whiteboards and pens
- Focus word cards
- The benefits of exercise resource per child

In a nutshell
Teacher subject knowledge for this unit:

The focus for this unit is re-visiting some of the spelling focuses from the Autumn term. Specifically, these are:
- the /i/ sound in the middle of a word spelled 'y'
- the /ai/ sound spelled 'ey'
- the prefixes *un-*, *dis-* and *mis-*
- doubling consonants at the end of a word when adding a suffix that starts with a vowel

Word list

gym	myth	they	grey	obey
unhappy	dislike	misbehave	running	sunny

1 Introduce/Review

- Ask the children to work in teams of six and to give themselves a team name.
- Explain that you are going to read a list of words aloud and that they should each write them down, thinking carefully about the correct spelling of every word, without discussing the spelling with their team mates.
- Read the focus words to the children, pronouncing them clearly. Once you have read all of the words and the children have written them down, involve them in spelling the words aloud accurately. Write up the correctly spelled words and ask them to check their own spellings and to add up their team's score, giving one mark for each correct spelling.
- Create a team scoreboard and record the number of marks that each team have scored. Display the scoreboard on the working wall.
- Discuss the challenges the children had when they were trying to spell the words. If necessary, explore some techniques and strategies they could use to help them the next time, e.g. visualising the word, visualising the tricky part of the word, saying the word syllable by syllable, thinking about root words. Write up each focus word as it is discussed and use highlighting and underlining to create a visual reminder of these strategies. Display the words on the working wall.

2 Teach

- Write up or display the focus words for the unit. Ask the children to work in pairs and to choose two words from the list that they think have a connection of some sort. Challenge them to explain that connection to another pair, e.g. spelling pattern such as 'y' in the middle of the words, the words have prefixes.
- If necessary, discuss the spelling focus for some of the words, e.g. words with the /i/ sound spelled 'y', doubling the consonant when adding a suffix beginning with a vowel.
- Re-visit the list of focus words and remind the children of the techniques they discussed for remembering how to spell the words. Focus on one of the words that the children found challenging. Ask the children to read it carefully then remove it from the list or cover it up and play Speedy spelling by asking the children to stand behind their chairs. Say the focus word and ask one child to say the first letter in the word, the next child should say the next letter in the word, and so on, until the word has been spelled. If a mistake is made, ask the child to sit down. Once the word is spelled, the children who remain standing call out 'Speedy spelling!' and sit down. You may wish to have a time limit in which the children have to spell each word.
- Ask the children to write down the focus words in their word books or spelling journals.

Spring term, Unit 1

> **Challenge!**
> Use the Spelling Fox Challenge: Who will win the spelling quiz? (1) to kick off or consolidate the learning. The children must help the Spelling Fox find the correct answers! Access online via My Rising Stars.

3 Practise

- Re-visit the focus words displayed on the working wall.
- As a class, discuss some of the spelling games and activities they have played that they have found helpful for learning and remembering how to spell words. If necessary, remind the children of some of these, e.g. Mind the gap, Living words, Word tennis.
- Ask the children to work in their teams of six to create two spelling activities that use the focus words for this unit. Make sure that any resources that they may need are available, e.g. whiteboards and pens, blank cards, paper.
- One they have developed their activities, they can split into mini-groups of three and try out their activities on another mini-group.
- Take feedback from the activities, encouraging the children to think about which activities they think really helped them to learn and remember how to spell the focus words.
- You may wish to give the teams a mark out of ten for originality, effectiveness or inventiveness for their activities and add these marks to the team scoreboard.

4 Apply

- Ask the children to work in their original teams of six.
- Re-visit the focus words for this unit, displayed on the working wall. Ask them to look carefully at the words, thinking about the reasons for the highlighting and underlining. Remove or cover up the words. Read out the words, one by one, asking the children to write them down without discussing how to spell the words with their team mates. Reveal the words and ask the children to check their spellings and to record how many they spelled correctly as individuals and as a team. Add the team scores to the scoreboard created earlier. Identify the winning team and invite them to share the strategies that they feel work for them with the rest of the class.

5 Review

- Give each child a copy of The benefits of exercise reading passage (see You will need) and ask them to read it through, thinking about what the missing words might be.
- Read the passage aloud, giving the children time to write in each missing word. Ask them to reread what they have written and to make any changes to their spelling of the missing words.
- Once they have done this, reveal the list of focus words for this unit and ask the children to swap their work with another team member and to check their spellings against the list. Ask the children to give the work they are marking a score out of ten and then to combine individual scores to create a team score. Add these marks to the team scoreboard and announce the overall winning team.

   The benefits of exercise

   Exercise is good for you, or so **they** say. One **sunny** day, I put on my new trainers and jogged down to the **gym**. First, I went on the **running** machine but it decided to **misbehave**. It went faster and faster until I fell off. I **dislike** that machine. Next, I tried the weights. They were too heavy and I dropped them on my foot. I was very **unhappy**. Finally, I tried rowing but the machine would not **obey** my instructions and I had to stop. I set off for home. The sky had turned **grey** and I ached all over. I decided that exercise is not good for you – it is a **myth**!

© 2016 Rising Stars UK Ltd.

Who will win the revision quiz?
Focus: review of Autumn term spellings

You will need:
Access online resources at My Rising Stars: www.risingstars-uk.com
- Group 1 focus word cards
- Group 2 focus word cards
- Group 3 focus word cards
- Group 4 focus word cards
- Group 5 focus word cards

In a nutshell
Teacher subject knowledge for this unit:
This unit gives you an opportunity to assess the children's knowledge of the content covered so far in the programme. The children take a revision quiz of the spellings and spelling rules.

> **Word list**
> Use a collection (or all) of the words from the Word banks within the Year 3, Autumn term of Rising Stars Spelling.

1 Introduce/Review

- Split the class into at least five groups and explain that they are each going to explore a spelling focus that they covered in the previous term. (If you would like the children to work in smaller groups, duplicate some of the sets of focus word cards, as appropriate.)
- Number the groups 1 to 5. Give each group their focus word cards (see You will need).
- Ask them to spread out their focus word cards on their tables and to read the words. Challenge them to work out what the spelling focus for their sets of cards is.
- Ask each group to feed back to the rest of the class, summarising their spelling focus.
- Monitor the accuracy of their summaries, correcting any misunderstandings if they arise. Ask each group to write out their summaries and display these, along with examples of relevant words, on the working wall.

2 Teach

- Ask each group to carry out an Open word sort activity with their cards. Explain that they can choose how to group their cards but must be able to explain how and why they sorted them in a particular way.
- If any groups require support, remind them of other word sort activities they have done and the criteria they used, e.g. by spelling pattern; alphabetically by first, second and third letter; by number of syllables; by word class.
- Ask each group to feed back on their open sorting activity to the rest of the class, explaining how they sorted their words and why they chose that way of sorting them.

3 Practise

- Ask each child in the class to choose two words from their group focus words. You may wish to mediate the choices that some children make to check that the words are appropriate for the activity.
- Ask the children to work in their groups and to play Guess my word by giving clues about their words. If necessary, demonstrate this, giving clues about word meaning, initial and/or final letter sounds, spelling patterns contained in the word, number of syllables.
- If the rest of the group struggle to guess the word, they are able to ask questions but only receive yes or no answers.

Spring term, Unit 2

Challenge!
Use the Spelling Fox Challenge: Who will win the revision quiz? to kick off or consolidate the learning. The children must help the Spelling Fox find the correct answers! Access online via My Rising Stars.

4 Apply

- Ask each child to choose two different words from their group focus words.
- They should take it in turns to read their words aloud clearly and challenge the rest of their group to write them down, spelling them accurately.
- Once every child has read their words, they can spell them aloud, allowing the rest of the group to check the accuracy of their spelling.
- Ask them to count up how many words they have spelled accurately and to record their score.

5 Review

- Within each group, give every child a number from 1 to 5 or 6, depending on the size of the group. Explain that all of the number 1s will work together, all of the number 2s will work together, etc.
- Ask each child to choose two words from their group focus words and to take them to their new group.
- Once the new groups have formed, every group member should teach the rest of the group their words, including any spelling rules or conventions.
- Each group can then carry out a quick-fire spelling activity where every child reads out their two words at some speed while the rest of the group write them down.
- Ask the children to count up how many words they have spelled accurately and to record their score. They can then add it to their score from the previous activity.
- Explore the range of scores that they have achieved, discussing with higher scorers what techniques they used to help them to spell accurately.

Can we spell words from our word list?

Focus: words from the Year 3/4 word list

You will need:
Access online resources at My Rising Stars: www.risingstars-uk.com
- Focus word cards
- Mind the gap resource per child

In a nutshell

Teacher subject knowledge for this unit:

The focus for this unit is on words taken from the statutory word list for Year 3/4. In addition to the well-established 'look, say, cover, write, check' strategy, children can use techniques that incorporate a range of learning styles, e.g. identifying the tricky bits of words, visualising the word and specific spelling patterns, pronouncing the words clearly and emphasising the syllables, chanting the spelling aloud, using actions, drawing images.

Word list

| decide | describe | different | difficult | disappear | early | earth |
| eight | eighth | enough | exercise | experience | experiment | extreme |

1 Introduce/Review

- Write up the following words:

decide	describe	different	difficult	disappear
early	earth	eight	enough	exercise
experience	experiment	extreme		

- Read the words aloud to the children, pronouncing them clearly, and explain that these are the words they are going to focus on in this unit, reminding them that they have come across some of the words before.
- Draw attention to the words *different* and *difficult* and remind them of the work they did on double consonants after a short vowel sound. Are they able to spot another word in the list that contains double consonants after a short vowel? (*disappear*)
- Focus on the words *decide* and *describe* and remind the children that these words contain split digraphs at the end (-*ide*, -*ibe*). Challenge them to spot other words in the list that end with a split digraph. (*exercise, extreme*)
- Focus on the word *eight* and remind the children that in one unit they looked at different ways of spelling the /ai/ sound. Write up the word *eighth* and establish that this is just one letter different from *eight* but it has a slightly different meaning. Challenge them to use the word *eighth* in a sentence.
- Give pairs of children the focus word cards and ask them to sort the words into groups in any way that they choose. Ask them to explain how they have grouped the words, why they chose those groupings and what they have learned about the words.
- Return to the focus word list and read the words aloud together. Check that the children are pronouncing the words accurately and clearly. Display the focus words on the working wall.

2 Teach

- Return to the list of focus words and read the first five (*decide, describe, different, difficult, disappear*) aloud, pronouncing them clearly. Ask the children to read them aloud with you.
- Discuss which parts of the words might be tricky to spell, e.g. the 'c' in *decide* and *describe*, the double consonants in *different, difficult* and *disappear*.
- Say the words, this time accentuating the individual letter sounds. Suggest to the children that saying the words like this might help them to remember how to spell the word correctly.

Spring term, Unit 3

Challenge!
Use the Spelling Fox Challenge: Can we spell words from our word list? (3) to kick off or consolidate the learning. The children must help the Spelling Fox find the correct answers! Access online via My Rising Stars.

- With the children, develop and write up five sentences that contain the focus words, e.g.
    a) I can't decide whether I prefer football or rugby.
    b) I will describe my house so that you know where I live.
    c) My best friends are twins but I think they look different.
    d) It is difficult to read when people are talking.
    e) At the magic show, we saw a rabbit disappear.
- Ask them to read the sentences, focus on the words, then close their eyes and picture the words.
- Involve them in spelling the five focus words aloud without looking at them. Write up the words and ask the children to check whether they are spelled correctly.
- Repeat this process with the rest of the focus words, grouping them into fours or fives. Once all of the words are written up correctly, read through the list, pronouncing them clearly, then reread them, accentuating the tricky parts of the words.

3 Practise

- Ask the children to work in pairs and to choose three or more of the focus words for this unit. Explain that they are going to create dictionary entries for each of their words.
- Show them an example of a dictionary entry and identify the features they should include, e.g. headword, word class, definition, example of a sentence containing the focus word.
- Choose one of the focus words and demonstrate how to create a dictionary entry for the word.
- Give the children time to create their own dictionary entries. Ask each pair to share their dictionary entries with another pair and comment constructively on each other's entries.
- Ask the children to make any changes to their entries in the light of the feedback they have received. Once they are happy with their entries, they can write them on large sheets of paper for display on the working wall, or in their word books or spelling journals.

4 Apply

- Give each child a copy of the Mind the gap activity (see You will need). Ask them to read the clues and fill in the gaps in each word with the correct letters. The letters in the shaded boxes will make a word from the focus word list.
- Once they have completed the activity, they can compare their answers with those of a friend.
- Establish whether there are any particular words, or parts of words, that are proving problematic and re-visit these. Write them up and, as a class, read each word and spell it aloud. Repeat this, increasing the pace each time.

5 Review

- Identify five or six words that the children are finding challenging.
- As a class, play Shannon's game, encouraging the children to think about, and visualise, the spelling patterns in the words. Remind them to think carefully about the letters that can and cannot come next as they predict the spelling of the words.
- Ask them to write the focus words in their word books or spelling journals and to check the accuracy of their spellings.
- Ask the children to work with a partner. They should each choose five words from the focus word list and take it in turns to challenge their partner to spell the words aloud. They can repeat this until they can both spell the words correctly.

How can we use prefixes?
Focus: prefix *re-*

You will need:
Access online resources at My Rising Stars: www.risingstars-uk.com
- Focus word cards
- Sentences resource per child
- Sentences (answers) for display

In a nutshell
Teacher subject knowledge for this unit:

This unit focuses on the impact of adding the prefix *re-* to a word. Prefixes are groups of letters that can be added to the beginning of a root word. They usually change the meaning of the root word. The prefix *re-* means *again* or *back*.

In this unit, the root words are recognisable actual words, e.g. *re-* + *act* = *react*, rather than root words that are derivations, e.g. *re-* + *peat* = *repeat*.

Word list

| redo | return | replay | refill | re-write |
| replace | recycle | reappear | rebuild | reposition |

1 Introduce/Review

- Before the start of the lesson, write up the focus words.
- Ask the children to read them silently to themselves and to work out what the spelling focus is. (*the prefix* re-) If necessary, remind them of the term *prefix*, explaining that it is a group of letters that goes at the front of the word and changes the meaning of the root word.
- Ask them to work with a partner and to try to work out what the prefix *re-* might mean. (*again or back*)
- Challenge each pair to produce a sentence orally that includes one of the focus words in order to demonstrate that they understand the meaning of the word. Once they have created their sentence, they can write it down and share it with another pair. Encourage each pair to comment constructively on each other's sentences, suggesting changes to help clarify the word meaning and to check the spelling of the focus word.
- Involve the children in writing up a summary of the spelling focus for this unit, making sure that it includes the definition of a prefix and the meaning of the prefix *re-*. Display this summary on the working wall.

2 Teach

- Split the class into five or six teams. Allocate five words from the Focus word cards (see You will need) to each team. Ask each team to create up to five clues for each of their focus words for use in a Guess my word activity. Remind them that the clues must not mention the word itself but they can refer to meaning, spelling patterns and word classes. Give each team member a number from 1 to 5 or 6, depending on numbers. Ask the teams to jigsaw so that all of the number 1s work together, all of the 2s work together, etc. and to take their Guess my word activities with them. They can then challenge each other, using the clues they have created.
- Take feedback from the activity, discussing which sort of clues were the most helpful in working out the words.

3 Practise

- Ask the children to work in their teams with the words they were allocated earlier.
- Ask each team member to choose one of the words and to read it carefully, thinking about any tricky parts of the word that might be problematic to spell. If necessary, remind them of techniques they can use to remember spellings, e.g. breaking the word down into syllables, pronouncing all of the letters, visualising the shape of the word, visualising

Spring term, Unit 4

Challenge!
Use the Spelling Fox Challenge: How can we use prefixes? (2) to kick off or consolidate the learning. The children must help the Spelling Fox find the correct answers! Access online via My Rising Stars.

spelling patterns. Ask them to practise spelling the word aloud and then writing it down until they can spell their word accurately. They should then teach each other their words until the whole team can spell all of their five words accurately.

- Ask every child to pair up with someone from another team who has *not* studied the same words as they have. They can then test each other on their five words.
- Take feedback from the activity. Check whether there are any particular words that are causing problems and note them down in order to follow up on them.

4 Apply

- Re-visit the list of words identified as causing problems. Write them up, involving the children in spelling them aloud. If possible, identify what the children find particularly tricky about the words and focus on those areas.
- Challenge the children to come up with some other words that start with the *re-* prefix. Are they able to differentiate between words that start with the *re-* prefix (*rebuild*) and words that start with the *re-* spelling pattern (*regular*)? If necessary, demonstrate how the prefix *re-* is added to a root word (*build*) whereas the word 'gular' (as in '*regular*') does not exist.
- Write up the following words and ask them to work out which have *re-* prefixes and which start with the spelling pattern *re-*:

    reach   reappear
    react   reason
    read   rebuild
    ready   recall
    really   replay

    Answers:

re- prefix	*re-* spelling pattern
react	reach
reappear	read
rebuild	ready
recall	really
replay	reason

- Challenge the children to work out the meanings of the words that start with the *re-* prefix, encouraging them to use each word in a sentence.

5 Review

- Give each child a copy of the Sentences resource (see You will need). Read each sentence aloud, saying the word in bold clearly, and ask the children to write in the missing words as you say them.

    Sentences
    a) Ellie liked to **recycle** things rather than throw them away.
    b) Dad wanted to **replay** the match so he could see the winning goal.
    c) Mum said she would go back to the shop and **return** my T-shirt.
    d) You can **refill** some bottles with water.
    e) She stayed in to re-write her homework.
    f) We need to **replace** the car because it has broken down.
    g) I saw the cat **reappear** on the other side of the wall.
    h) I will **reposition** the picture because it's crooked.
    i) My teacher said I had to **redo** my spellings.
    j) We had to **rebuild** the shed after the accident.

Can we make our spelling super?
Focus: prefix *super-*

You will need:
Access online resources at My Rising Stars: www.risingstars-uk.com
- Bingo cards
- A4 paper and pens

In a nutshell
Teacher subject knowledge for this unit:

Prefixes are groups of letters that are added to the beginning of a root word. They usually change the meaning of the root word. The prefix *super-* means *over and above*, or *bigger and better*. This unit teaches children about using the prefix *super-*.

Word list			
supermarket	superman	superpower	superhuman
superstar	supersonic	superstore	

1 Introduce/Review

- Ask the children to tell you what they know about prefixes and to give you some examples of prefixes that they have come across. Establish that adding a prefix to a word changes its meaning and sometimes changes its spelling.
- Write up the following words:

    man   hero   power

    and the following prefixes:

    anti-   re-   super-

- Challenge the children to decide which prefix could be added to every word to make a new word. (*super-*) Take feedback and guide the children towards choosing *super-* by trying out each prefix with each word to test whether it creates a word that the children recognise. Write up the new words:

    superman   superhero   superpower

- Ask the children to use each word in a sentence in order to show that they understand the meanings. Establish that the prefix *super-* means *over and above*, or *bigger and better*. It is added to the beginning of root words, with no space or hyphen, to make a new word. Summarise the spelling focus for this unit and display it on the working wall.

2 Teach

- Remind the children that the spelling focus is the prefix *super-* and that it means *over and above*, or *bigger and better*.
- Ask the children to work in pairs and give a bingo card to each pair. Explain that you are going to read aloud the definition of a word, and if they have that word on their bingo card, they should cross it out. The first pair to cross out all of their words should call out 'Bingo!' (Note that it is possible for more than one pair to complete their cards at the same time.)

    Definitions
    A self-service shop selling groceries. (*supermarket*)
    A person with amazing powers. (*superman*)
    Amazing skill or ability. (*superpower*)
    More than is possible for a human being. (*superhuman*)
    A very famous person. (*superstar*)
    Faster than the speed of sound. (*supersonic*)
    An enormous shop. (*superstore*)

- Once the children have mastered the game, they can work in groups of five or six and repeat the bingo game, with one child acting as caller.

Spring term, Unit 5

Challenge!
Use the Spelling Fox Challenge: Can we make our spelling super? to kick off or consolidate the learning. The children must help the Spelling Fox find the correct answers! Access online via My Rising Stars.

3 Practise

- Ask the children to tell what they know about the prefix *super-* and to give you some examples of words that begin with that prefix, e.g. *supermarket, superpower*.
- Establish that the prefix *super-* can be added to many words to create new words. Explain that new words are being invented all of the time and that every year some of those new words are allowed into the dictionary – as long as they have been used regularly by a large number of people.
- Suggest to the children that they create their own class superdictionary by inventing words that start with the prefix *super-*.
- Ask them how the words in dictionaries are organised. (*alphabetically*) Together, look at pages from dictionaries to explore how they are laid out. List the features on a large sheet of paper, e.g. the main entries are in bold; it says what word class the word is, e.g. noun, adjective; there is a definition of the word.
- Ask the children to work in pairs to invent three new words that start with the prefix *super-*. They should then decide what word class they belong to and create a definition. Once they are happy with their words, they can share them with another pair. In their foursomes, the children should reduce their joint list of six words to two words, by deciding which words they would use most often.
- Ask the groups to write each of their words on an A4 sheet of paper, along with the word class and definition.
- Take feedback from the activity and display the new superwords on the working wall.

4 Apply

- Re-visit the new superwords list on the working wall. Involve the children in organising the words into alphabetical order in order to produce a superdictionary.
- Ask them to choose their two favourite words and to use them in a single supersentence.
- Give each child the chance to share their sentence with the inventors of the superwords in order to check that the words have been used in a way that makes sense.
- Ask them to polish their supersentences and to write them out in their word books or spelling journals.
- Challenge them to try to use some of their superwords during the day – in the playground, during lunch break – and to see if they can persuade other people (children and adults) to start using them too.

5 Review

- Ask the children to share their experiences of using their superwords at school and at home. Did they convince anyone that they were real words or to start using them?
- As a class, re-visit the summarised spelling focus for this unit, displayed on the working wall, and ask them to tell you what they think they have learned during this unit.

Can you correct your own writing?

Focus: words from children's own writing

You will need:
Access online resources at My Rising Stars: www.risingstars-uk.com
- Word books or spelling journals
- Dictionaries
- A4 whiteboards and pens

In a nutshell

Teacher subject knowledge for this unit:

This unit focuses on words that the children identify as incorrectly spelled in their own writing.

Following discussion on strategies for remembering how to spell specific words, the children use an approach to practise and reinforce spelling. The focus words are re-visited a number of times through various activities, giving the children the opportunity to read and reread the words, as well as writing them down and using them in sentences.

> **Word list**
> Identified by the children from their own writing.

1 Introduce/Review

- Ask the children to look through any writing they have done in English, and in other subjects, and to find up to ten words that they have spelled incorrectly. These may well be words that have already been identified by you during marking. Some children might need adult support in identifying these words.
- Ask them to draw up a 'look, say, cover, write, check' table in their word books or spelling journals and to write their focus words in the left-hand column. They should then check that they have spelled them correctly by asking a friend, an adult, reading the marking comments or checking in a dictionary.
- Ask them to work in pairs and to read their lists to each other, discussing what the words mean and which parts of the words they find particularly tricky to spell.

2 Teach

- As a class, discuss techniques that the children can use to remember spellings, e.g. pronouncing all of the letters in a word, including those that are silent; visualising whole words and letter patterns; spotting words within words; breaking words down into root words and prefixes/suffixes.
- Ask them to carry out the 'look, say, cover, write, check' process with each of the words on their lists, completing the table in their word books or spelling journals. You may wish to put a time limit on the activity to focus the children's attention on the task.
- Once they have completed their 'look, say, cover, write, check' tables, they can check with a partner that they have spelled the words accurately. If there is any dispute, they can check in a dictionary.

3 Practise

- Ask the children to re-present their original word lists as two separate columns: those they *did* spell correctly after the 'look, say, cover, write, check' approach, and those they *did not*. They could use a tick or a cross as the heading for the relevant list. Make sure that the words originally spelled incorrectly are spelled correctly on the new list.
- Ask them to work in pairs and give each pair two whiteboards and pens. Explain that they are going to practise spelling their challenging words (the words they misspelled) by taking it in turns to say a word and asking their partner to write it down on their whiteboard. They can then check the spelling against their word lists.
- As a follow up, they can read a word together and spell it aloud. Encourage them to develop a rhythm and build up speed with this so that it becomes a memorable chant.

Spring term, Unit 6

Challenge!

Use the Spelling Fox Challenge: Can you correct your own writing? (3) to kick off or consolidate the learning. The children must help the Spelling Fox find the correct answers! Access online via My Rising Stars.

4 Apply

- Ask the children to continue to work with their partners and to each choose five words from their original lists. They can then combine their words so that each pair has a collection of ten focus words.
- Challenge them to work together and to read and write the list of words, with the aim of reducing the number of incorrectly spelled words every time they go through the list. Some children might benefit from a time limit on the activity.
- At the end of the session, ask how many incorrectly spelled words each pair of children have left on their lists.

5 Review

- Ask the children to return to their own individual spelling lists created at the beginning of this unit and to swap them with a partner.
- They should read out each word on their partner's list, giving their partner time to write the words down correctly but maintaining a steady pace.
- Once each child has had the opportunity to write down their words correctly, they should check each other's lists.
- Ask them to develop and write sentences that include their focus words to show that they understand the meanings of the words.

How can we use prefixes?

Focus: the prefixes *anti-* and *sub-*

You will need:
Access online resources at My Rising Stars: www.risingstars-uk.com
- About three copies of the Find my family cards
- A4 whiteboards and pens
- Making new words resource per child
- Missing words resource per child

In a nutshell

Teacher subject knowledge for this unit:

Prefixes are groups of letters that can be added to the beginning of root words. They usually change the meaning of the root word. The focus prefixes for this unit are *anti-* and *sub-*. The prefix *anti-* means *against*. The prefix *sub-* means *under* or *below*.

Word list

antifreeze	antisocial	antiseptic	anticlockwise	subheading	
submarine	subtitle	subdivide	subset	substandard	subway

1 Introduce/Review

- Explain to the children that the spelling focus for this unit is prefixes. Ask them to remind you what a prefix is (*a group of letters that can be added to the beginning of a root word*) and what it does (*it changes the meaning of the root word*). Write up the following words:

antifreeze	subheading	subset
antisocial	submarine	substandard
antiseptic	subtitle	subway
anticlockwise	subdivide	

- Challenge the children to work out which prefixes they are going to explore (*sub-* and *anti-*). Discuss the words and their meanings, asking them to use some of the words in sentences.
- Establish that the prefix *sub-* means *under* or *below* and the prefix *anti-* means *against*. Elaborate on this explanation by illustrating with an example, e.g. a submarine is a ship that can travel under water: *sub* means *under*, the word *marine* is related to the sea.
- Ask them to discuss some of the other words with a partner. Are they able to work out the meanings by looking at the prefix and root word separately?
- Summarise the spelling focus for this unit, e.g. 'A prefix is a group of letters that can be added to the beginning of a root word. The prefix *anti-* means *against*. The prefix *sub-* means *under* or *below*.' Display this summary on the working wall.

2 Teach

- Give out the multiple sets of the Find my family cards (see You will need) so that each child has a card. Ask the children to read their word and to practise saying it aloud clearly to themselves.
- They can then move around the room, saying their word aloud, pronouncing it clearly and listening for other children saying a word that starts with the same prefix. Once they have found their family, they should sit down as a group.
- Give each group an A4 whiteboard and pens. Ask each group to develop four or five sentences that each include one of the words. Once they are happy with their sentences, they can write them on their whiteboards and hold them up.
- Quickly check the whiteboards to make sure that the families do consist of words with the same prefix and that the words have been used accurately in the sentences.
- Read some of the sentences aloud to emphasise the meanings of the prefixes *sub-* and *anti-*.

Spring term, Unit 7

Challenge!
Use the Spelling Fox Challenge: How can we use prefixes? (3) to kick off or consolidate the learning. The children must help the Spelling Fox find the correct answers! Access online via My Rising Stars.

3 Practise

- Ask the children to work in groups of three. Give each group an A4 whiteboard and pen and the Making new words resource (see You will need).
- Explain that they should choose a root word from the Making new words sheet, read it and discuss what it means, then write it on their whiteboard and experiment with adding the two prefixes to the root word. They can then read the resulting new words. They should decide which of the two new words is a real word, again discussing the meaning and testing it by trying it out in a sentence.
- Once they have decided which prefix goes with a particular word, they should write the new word under the relevant heading on the Making new words sheet.
- Take feedback from the activity and write up the correctly spelled new words. Ask the children to write these in their word books or spelling journals.

4 Apply

- Give each child a copy of the Missing words resource (see You will need).
- Explain that they should read each sentence and then choose which word would work best in the gap. One they have decided on the missing word, they can write it into the gap, checking their spelling carefully.
- Ask the children to work in pairs and to check which words they have each written in the gap. If they have written something different, they should discuss which word they think is correct, and why, and make a decision on which word they are going to opt for.

5 Review

- Ask the children to remind you of the focus for this unit. Write up the two prefixes *sub-* and *anti-* and discuss their meanings. Write these next to the relevant prefix.
- Ask the children to work in pairs. Explain that they are going to try to invent some new words. Each pair should choose one of the prefixes and try to create at least five new words. They can then use their new words in sentences.
- Ask each pair to join another pair and to share their sentences. Challenge the new pair to write a definition of the new words.

© 2016 Rising Stars UK Ltd.

How can we use prefixes?

Focus: prefix *auto-*

You will need:
Access online resources at My Rising Stars: www.risingstars-uk.com
- Pairs word cards
- The Newsreader resource per child

In a nutshell

Teacher subject knowledge for this unit:

Prefixes are groups of letters that can be added to the beginning of root words. They usually change the meaning of the root word. The prefix *auto-* means *self*.

Word list				
automobile	autograph	autobiography	autocue	automatic

1 Introduce/Review

- Before the start of this unit, write up the following sentences:
    a) Dad jumped into the automobile and drove off up the road.
    b) My favourite player signed my autograph book at the match.
    c) In his autobiography, he wrote about his life before he became famous.
    d) The newsreader couldn't carry on when the autocue stopped working.
    e) In our street, there is a house with automatic gates that open when a car drives up to them.
- Read the sentences aloud to the children. Challenge them to spot something that one word in each sentence has in common. (*the prefix auto-*)
- Involve individual children in underlining both the word with the prefix *auto-* in each sentence and the prefix itself; you may wish to use two colours for this underlining activity.
- Reread each sentence, focusing on the word with the *auto-* prefix. Discuss the meaning of each word, supporting the children in working it out from the root word, the context of the sentence and the meaning of the prefix *auto-* (*self*).
- Write up each word, along with the definition, and display them on the working wall, e.g.
    a) automobile – an *automobile* is a car.
    b) autograph – an *autograph* is the signature of a famous person.
    c) autobiography – an *autobiography* is the story of someone's life that a they have written themselves.
    d) autocue – an *autocue* is a piece of equipment that shows the words a newsreader should read.
    e) automatic – *automatic* means something that happens without a person needing to do it.
- Check that the children are able to identify the prefix in each word.

2 Teach

- Ask the children to tell you about some other prefixes that they have been working on recently, e.g. *re-, super-, anti-, sub-*. Challenge them to tell you some words that start with these prefixes. Are they able to explain what the prefixes mean?
    - ✓ *re-* = again or back
    - ✓ *super-* = over and above, bigger and better
    - ✓ *anti-* = against
    - ✓ *sub-* = under or below
- Encourage them to use some of the words in sentences to demonstrate their understanding of the word meanings.

Spring term, Unit 8

Challenge!
Use the Spelling Fox Challenge: How can we use prefixes? (4) to kick off or consolidate the learning. The children must help the Spelling Fox find the correct answers! Access online via My Rising Stars.

3 Practise

- Ask the children to work in pairs. Give each pair sets of 10–20 cards from the Pairs word cards (see You will need), making sure that there are matching pairs within the sets.
- Ask them to play Pairs by laying out their cards face down on the table in front of them. Each child takes it in turn to choose a card. Once they have their card, they should turn over another card. If the prefix on that card matches that on their original card, they keep it and repeat until they no longer find a pair. The other child then takes their turn. They repeat this until they have collected all of the cards. The winner is the child with the most pairs of cards.
- Remind them to try to remember the cards that they have replaced face down on the table in order to find them when it is their turn.

4 Apply

- Ask the children, in their pairs, to choose three of the Pairs word cards and to orally create three sentences that each contains one of the words.
- Once they are happy with their sentences, they can write them down.
- Ask each pair to join with another pair and to check each other's sentences for both meaning and spelling.
- In their groups of four, ask them to carry out a mini spelling test. One child can take on the role of tester and give the rest of the group the spellings and check the accuracy of the answers.
- Ask them to record their focus words accurately in their word books or spelling journals.

5 Review

- Give each child a copy of The Newsreader resource (see You will need). Read the passage to the children, asking them to write in the missing words in the gaps.
- Ask each child to swap their completed passages with a partner and check the spellings of the missing words.

The Newsreader

I **returned** to the building in a luxury **automobile** that drove though the **subway** to the studio. Then I walked through the **automatic** doors past the fans who were waiting for my **autograph**.

I sat at my desk and looked through the script for the programme.
The **autocue** sprang into life, scrolling through the script. I **reread** the words that I was going to deliver to camera. I wondered how the audience would **react** to the story. The news that **Superman** had used his **superpowers** to defeat the enemy would soon be **released**. And I was the person who would **retell** that story to the world.

How can we use prefixes?
Focus: prefix *inter-*

You will need:
Access online resources at My Rising Stars: www.risingstars-uk.com
- Dictionaries
- Bingo cards

In a nutshell
Teacher subject knowledge for this unit:
Prefixes are groups of letters that can be added to the beginning of root words. They usually change the meaning of the root word. The prefix *inter-* means *between*.

Word list

| international | interview | intercom | interfere | interrupt | interval |

1 Introduce/Review

- Remind the children of the work they have done this term on prefixes. Ask them to remind you what a prefix is (*a group of letters that goes at the beginning of a root word*) and what it does (*it changes the meaning of the root word*).
- Write up the following words:

    international   *interview*   *intercom*

- Challenge them to identify the prefix in the words. (*inter-*) Explain that it means *between*. Explore the meanings of the words that you have listed. If necessary, use the words in sentences to support the children in identifying the word meanings, e.g.
    a) England and Germany played each other in an international football match.
    b) I had an interview to see if I was suitable for the job.
    c) I can use the intercom to talk to someone outside the front door.
- If appropriate, explain that the 'com' part of the word *intercom* is short for *communicate*.

2 Teach

- Ask the children to tell you about some other prefixes that they have been working on recently, e.g. *re-, super-, anti-, sub-, auto-*. Challenge them to tell you some words that start with these prefixes. Are they able to explain what the prefixes mean?
    ✓ *re-* = again or back
    ✓ *super-* = over and above, bigger and better
    ✓ *anti-* = against
    ✓ *sub-* = under or below
    ✓ *auto-* = self
- Encourage them to use some of the words in sentences to demonstrate their understanding of the word meanings.

3 Practise

- Explain to the children that they are going to use their dictionaries to find the meanings of some words. Ask them to remind you how a dictionary is organised. (*alphabetically by first letter*)
- With the children, discuss the techniques that they can use to look up words quickly in a dictionary, e.g. identifying the first letter and opening the dictionary to where they think that letter might be; identifying the second letter in the word and finding that group of words in the dictionary.
- Establish that many dictionaries also tell you what word class a word belongs to. If appropriate, demonstrate this, asking the children to follow as you find a word in a dictionary. Identify the word class and the meaning of the word.

Spring term, Unit 9

Challenge!
Use the Spelling Fox Challenge: How can we use prefixes? (5) to kick off or consolidate the learning. The children must help the Spelling Fox find the correct answers! Access online via My Rising Stars.

- Write up the following words that start with the prefix *inter-*:

    interfere   *interior*   *internal*   *interrupt*   *interval*

- Ask them to work in pairs to carry out a Speedy search activity for the words in their dictionaries. They can then write down the word, its word class and the meaning.
- You may wish to ask some children to then use the word in a sentence.
- Take feedback from the activity.
- Draw attention to the fact that in the words they have been investigating, they might not recognise the root words as they are not necessarily complete words. If appropriate, explain that this could be because they are shortened versions of a word (as in *intercom*) or a word from a language other than English (as in *interrupt* – from the Latin *rumpere*, which means *to break*).

4 Apply

- Ask the children to work in pairs and give each pair a bingo card (see You will need).
- Explain that you are going to read aloud a list of words and if they have that word on their bingo card, they should cross it out. The first pair to cross out all of their words should call out 'Bingo!' (Note that it is possible for more than one pair to complete their cards at the same time.)

    Words

international	*reappear*	*rebuild*
automatic	*interfere*	*superpower*
subway	*supermarket*	*anticlockwise*
antifreeze	*interrupt*	*submarine*
interview	*interval*	*autograph*

- Discuss any techniques that the winning team(s) used to find the words quickly, e.g. visualising the whole word, thinking about and visualising spelling patterns.

5 Review

- Re-visit the various prefixes explored this term (*re-*, *super-*, *anti-*, *sub-*, *auto-* and *inter-*). Ask the children to remind you of the meaning of each prefix.
- Ask them to work in pairs and to use their dictionaries to find up to three words that start with each of the prefixes.
- As the children find them, they can write them down, along with their word classes and meanings. Challenge some children to record words that they have not previously come across.
- Take feedback from the activity. Explore any new words that the children have found and involve them in using the words in sentences.
- Challenge them to invent some words of their own using the prefix *inter-*, to develop some definitions and then use the new words in a sentence, e.g. '*Interclass* means *between classes*. The school held an interclass spelling competition.'

What are homophones?
Focus: homophones and near-homophones

You will need:
Access online resources at My Rising Stars: www.risingstars-uk.com
- A4 whiteboards and pens
- Dictionaries
- Loop game cards

In a nutshell

Teacher subject knowledge for this unit:

Homophones are words that sound the same but are spelled differently and have different meanings.

Word list

ball	bawl	break	brake
groan	grown	fair	fare
heel	heal	grate	great
berry	bury	hear	here

1 Introduce/Review

- Explain to the children that the focus for this unit is homophones, and that these are words that sound the same but have different meanings and are spelled differently.
- Write up three pairs of words to illustrate what homophones are, e.g.

ball	bawl
groan	grown
heel	heal

- Read each word aloud, pronouncing them clearly and asking the children to repeat the words.
- Explore the different meanings of the pairs of words by using them in sentences, e.g.
    a) It made the baby bawl when she lost her ball.
    b) Mum gave a groan when she saw that I had grown out of my uniform.
    c) I hoped that the cut on my heel would heal soon.
- Discuss the meanings of the words.
- Give dictionaries to pairs of children. Ask them to remind you what a dictionary is used for (*to find out how words are spelled and what they mean*) and how the words are organised (*alphabetically*). Discuss how they would look up two words that start with the same letter (*by looking at the second and, if necessary, third letters*).
- Focus on the pair of words *ball* and *bawl*. Demonstrate how to look them up in the dictionary, asking the children to follow what you are doing. Remind them that the letter 'b' is very close to the beginning of the alphabet, so they should open the dictionary near the front but not on the first page. Discuss the word meanings once you have found them.
- Repeat this activity with the words *groan* and *grown*, *heel* and *heal*.

2 Teach

- Write up the following pair of homophones:

  berry   bury

- Explain to the children that you are going to read out two definitions and that they should discuss these with a partner and decide which definition fits which word.
    ✓ Definition 1: a fruit on a bush or tree.
    ✓ Definition 2: to put something in a hole in the ground.
- Give each pair of children an A4 whiteboard and ask them to write down the two words. Once they have made their decision on what each word means, they should write the definition numbers next to the relevant word on their whiteboards.

Spring term, Unit 10

> **Challenge!**
> Use the Spelling Fox Challenge: What are homophones? to kick off or consolidate the learning. The children must help the Spelling Fox find the correct answers! Access online via My Rising Stars.

- Ask each pair to hold up their whiteboards and take a vote on which definition goes with which word.
- Check their decisions by looking up the words in a dictionary.
- Repeat this activity with two further homophones, e.g. *break* and *brake*.
  - ✓ Definition 1: to stop or slow down.
  - ✓ Definition 2: to damage something.
- Once the vote has been taken, again encourage them to check the word meanings in their dictionaries.

3 Practise

- Write up three further pairs of homophones:

fair	*fare*
grate	*great*
hear	*here*

- If necessary, write up sentences that include the words, e.g.
  a) Jack paid the fare when he caught the bus on the way to the fair.
  b) The metal grate looked great in the fireplace.
  c) I hear that it took you a long time to get here because of the heavy traffic.
- Ask the children, in their pairs, to look up the homophones in their dictionaries and to write down the words and their meanings.
- Write up a selection of homophones that children have been introduced to in this unit, e.g. *ball, bawl*; *heel, heal*; *break, brake*.
- Ask each pair of children to join with another pair to carry out a Speedy search activity in their dictionaries by choosing one of the focus words and looking them up as quickly as they can. Encourage them to keep a tally as to who finds the word first in each case. Ask the 'winner' in each team to report back to the rest of the class about the techniques they used that helped them to find the words quickly.

4 Apply

- Play Shannon's game by writing up the first letter of one of the focus words from the unit and encouraging the children to spell the rest of the word, letter by letter. Remind them to think about spelling patterns to work out which letters could come next in each case.
- Repeat this activity with the homophone related to the word.

5 Review

- Use the Loop game cards (see You will need) to focus the children on the word meanings of the homophones.
- Ask the children to work in pairs. Give out a card to each pair of children. Start the game by choosing a pair to read the definition at the bottom. The pair with the correct linked word at the top of their card should read it out and then read the definition at the bottom of their card.
- Once the game is complete, repeat it two or three times, challenging the children to speed up each time.

Can we spell words from our word list?

Focus: words from the Year 3/4 word list

You will need:
Access online resources at My Rising Stars: www.risingstars-uk.com
- Bingo cards
- A4 whiteboards and pens
- Focus word cards
- Crossword
- A grammar guide resource per child
- A grammar guide (answers) for display

In a nutshell

Teacher subject knowledge for this unit:

The words for this unit are taken from the statutory word list for Year 3/4.

Word list				
famous	favourite	February	forward	fruit
grammar	group	guard	guide	

1 Introduce/Review

- Ask the children to work in pairs. Give each pair a bingo card (see You will need). Explain that you are going to read out a list of words and that they should listen carefully and, when they hear a word that is on their bingo cards, they should cross it out. Once they have crossed out every word on their card, they should call out 'Bingo!' The first pair to cross out all of their words are the winners. (Note that it is possible for more than one pair to complete their cards at the same time.)
- You may wish to set a further challenge to produce an overall winner, such as giving a definition and asking the children to identify which of their words the definition refers to.

2 Teach

- Write up the words that begin with the letter 'f':

    famous   *favourite*   *February*   *forward*   *fruit*

- Read each word, pronouncing it clearly, and asking the children to repeat it after you. Discuss which parts of each word the children think they might find tricky to spell, e.g. the 'ou' spelling pattern in *famous* and *favourite*; the 'uar' spelling pattern in *February*.
- Focus on each word in turn. Encourage the children to say the word aloud clearly and to visualise the word, particularly the tricky part. Then ask them to spell it aloud as you write it down. Encourage them to build up to chanting the spelling so that it becomes embedded and automatic.
- Repeat this process with the words beginning with the letter 'g':

    grammar   *group*   *guard*   *guide*

3 Practise

- Write up the focus words. Read them and ask the children to read the list, pointing to words at random.
- Give each child in the class an A4 whiteboard and pen. Give them one last chance to look at the focus words then delete or hide them.
- Carry out a Show me activity by saying some of the focus words aloud, pronouncing them clearly, and asking the children to write them on their whiteboards and to hold them up to show you. Use this as an opportunity to check the accuracy of individual children's spelling.
- Once they have completed the activity, ask whether there are any words that are still causing them problems.
- Write up these words and identify which parts of each word they are struggling with. You may wish to carry out a Shannon's game activity with these words to reinforce their spellings.

Spring term, Unit 11

Challenge!

Use the Spelling Fox Challenge: Can we spell words from our word list? (4) to kick off or consolidate the learning. The children must help the Spelling Fox find the correct answers! Access online via My Rising Stars.

4 Apply

- Remind the children of the focus words for this unit by holding up the focus word cards (see You will need) and asking them to read them aloud.
- Choose three or four of the words. Hold them up one by one and ask the children to tell you the word class of the word, e.g. *famous* is an adjective, *group* is a noun. They should then try to use it in a sentence. Challenge them to include two of the words in one sentence, and then three.
- Give children the crossword (see You will need) and ask them to read the clues and to fill in the gaps, checking that they are spelling the words accurately.

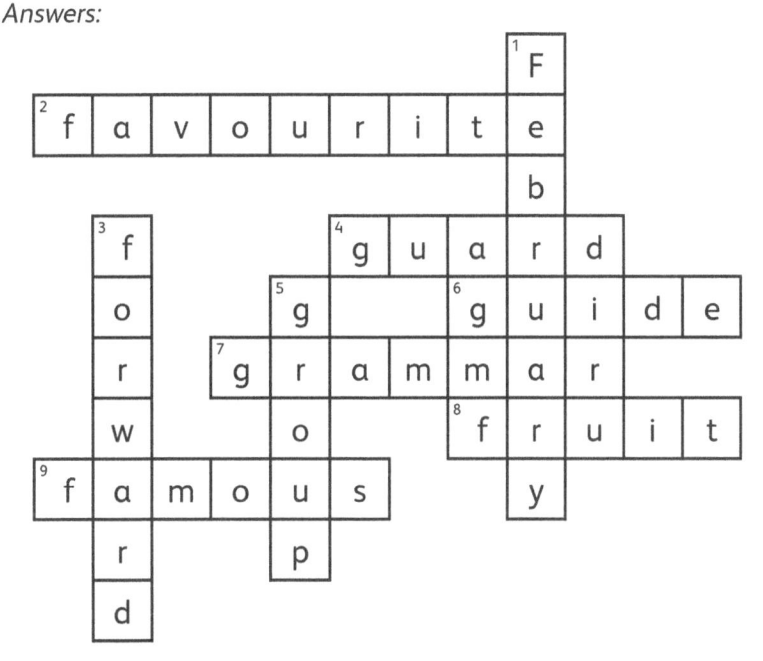

Answers:

							¹F			
²f	a	v	o	u	r	i	t	e		
							b			
	³f			⁴g	u	a	r	d		
	o		⁵g		⁶g	u	i	d	e	
	r		⁷g	r	a	m	m	a	r	
	w		o			⁸f	r	u	i	t
⁹f	a	m	o	u	s		y			
	r		p							
	d									

5 Review

- Give individual children a copy of the grammar guide resource (see You will need) and ask them to read it through. Read the passage aloud to the children, asking them to write in the missing words.

   A grammar guide

   It was in **February** that I became **famous** for writing the best-selling **guide** to **grammar**. Every day, the children in my class looked **forward** to learning more about their **favourite** subject. Unfortunately, there was one **group** who did not understand grammar and they said that the word **fruit** could not be a noun and a verb. I told them it could and so could the word **guard**.

Can you correct your own writing?

Focus: words from children's own writing

You will need:
Access online resources at My Rising Stars: www.risingstars-uk.com
- Dictionaries
- Word books or spelling journals
- Bean bags

In a nutshell

Teacher subject knowledge for this unit:

This unit focuses on words that the children identify as incorrectly spelled in their own writing. Following discussion on strategies for remembering how to spell specific words, the 'look, say, cover, write, check' approach is used to practise and reinforce spellings. The focus words are re-visited a number of times through various approaches, giving children the opportunity to read and reread the words, as well as writing them down and using them in sentences.

> **Word list**
>
> Identified by the children from their own writing.

1 Introduce/Review

- Ask the children to look through any writing they have done in English, and in other subjects, and to find up to ten words that they have spelled incorrectly. These may well be words that have already been identified by you during marking. Some children might need adult support in identifying these words.
- Ask them to draw up a 'look, say, cover, write, check' table in their word books or spelling journals and to write their focus words in the left-hand column. They should then check that they have spelled them correctly by asking a friend, an adult, reading the marking comments or checking in a dictionary.
- Ask them to work in pairs and to read their lists to each other, discussing what the words mean and which parts of the words they find particularly tricky to spell.

2 Teach

- As a class, discuss techniques that the children can use to remember spellings, e.g. pronouncing all of the letters in a word, including those that are silent; visualising whole words and letter patterns; spotting words within words; breaking words down into root words and prefixes/suffixes.
- Ask them to carry out the 'look, say, cover, write, check' process with each of the words on their lists, completing the table in their word books or spelling journals. You may wish to put a time limit on the activity to focus the children's attention on the task.
- Once the children have completed their 'look, say, cover, write, check' tables, they can check with a partner that they have spelled the words accurately. If there is any dispute, they can check in a dictionary.

3 Practise

- Ask them to re-present their original word lists as two separate columns: those they *did* spell correctly after the 'look, say, cover, write, check' approach, and those they *did not*. They could use a tick or a cross as the heading for the relevant list.
- Ask the children to work in pairs and give each pair a bean bag. Ask them to choose a word from their incorrectly spelled list, to read it and then carry out a Word tennis activity, spelling the word letter by letter, passing the bean bag to each other as they say each letter. They can repeat this with other words from their lists.

Spring term, Unit 12

Challenge!
Use the Spelling Fox Challenge: Can you correct your own writing? (4) to kick off or consolidate the learning. The children must help the Spelling Fox find the correct answers! Access online via My Rising Stars.

4 Apply

- Ask the children to continue to work with their partners and to each choose five words from their original lists. They can then combine their words so that each pair has a collection of ten focus words.
- Challenge them to choose at least five words from their collection and to produce sentences that contain those five words. They can write out those sentences, leaving gaps for the focus words. They can then join up with another pair and swap their sentences, reading them aloud to each other and writing in the missing words. They can check each other's spelling of the missing words.

5 Review

- Ask the children to return to their own individual spelling lists created at the beginning of this unit and to swap them with a partner.
- They should read out each word on their partner's list, giving their partner time to write the words down correctly but maintaining a steady pace.
- Once each child has had the opportunity to write down their words correctly, they should check each other's lists.
- Ask them to develop and write sentences that include their focus words to show that they understand the meanings of the words.

Who will win the spelling quiz?
Focus: review of Spring term spellings

You will need:
Access online resources at My Rising Stars: www.risingstars-uk.com
- Focus word cards
- A small ball
- A4 whiteboards and pens
- Prefixes resource per child
- Prefixes (answers) for display

In a nutshell
Teacher subject knowledge for this unit:

The focus for this unit is re-visiting some of the spelling focuses from the Spring term. Specifically, these are using the prefixes *re-* (meaning *back*), *super-* (meaning *over and above*, or *bigger and better*), *anti-* (meaning *against*) and *sub-* (meaning *under or below*).

Word list				
return	refill	replace	superman	superpower
superstar	antisocial	anticlockwise	subway	submarine

1 Introduce/Review

- Explain to the children that they are going to take part in a Guess my word activity. Write up the numbers 1 to 5 and explain that they will start with five points but every time they do not guess the word correctly, they will lose a point. Read out the five clues below and ask the children to see if they can work out what the word is.
    1) This word starts with a prefix.
    2) It starts with the 19th letter of the alphabet, which is a consonant.
    3) It is a noun.
    4) It has three syllables.
    5) It means someone with amazing powers.
- Write up the word (*superman*) and the score.
- Repeat the Guess my word activity with the word *anticlockwise* and these clues:
    1) This word starts with a prefix.
    2) It starts with the first letter of the alphabet.
    3) It is a noun.
    4) It has four syllables.
    5) It means to go in the opposite direction to a clock's hands.
- Again, write up the word and the score.
- Challenge the children to notice what the two words have in common. (*They both start with prefixes.*)
- Explore the children's understanding of prefixes. Are they able to tell you what a prefix is, what effect it has when it is added to a word, and can they give any examples of words that start with prefixes?
- Summarise the discussion with a definition of a prefix, e.g. 'A group of letters that can be added to the beginning of a root word. Prefixes usually change the meaning of the root word.' Display this definition on the working wall.

2 Teach

- Ask the children to work in groups of five or six. Give each group a set of focus word cards (see You will need) and ask them to lay the cards out, face down, on the table in front of them.
- Ask each child in the group to pick up one of the word cards and to read it, without letting anyone else in their group see the word. They should write down five clues for their word. Groups can then play Guess my word, with each child taking it in turns to read out the clues for their word.
- Take feedback from the activity, asking some children to read out their clues and others to explain which clues had given them the most help in working out a word.

Summer term, Unit 1

> **Challenge!**
> Use the Spelling Fox Challenge: Who will win the spelling quiz? (2) to kick off or consolidate the learning. The children must help the Spelling Fox find the correct answers! Access online via My Rising Stars.

- Write up or display the full list of the focus words for this unit. Challenge the children to identify and underline the four prefixes that are used in the focus words. Display the words, with the prefixes underlined, on the working wall.

3 Practise

- Take the children into a large open space such as the hall or playground. Ask them to sit in a circle.
- Carry out a whole class Letter tennis activity by showing and then saying one of the focus words. You may wish to start off the activity yourself by saying the initial letter and then rolling the ball to one of the children. The child receiving the ball says the next letter of the word and passes the ball to another child, and so on. Write up the letters that the children say until they finish the word. Ask them to check the accuracy of their spelling of the word.

4 Apply

- Refer to the display of focus words with underlined prefixes on the working wall. Discuss with the children what the prefixes mean. Write up the prefixes and their meanings: *re-* (meaning *back*), *super-* (meaning *over and above*, or *bigger and better*), *anti-* (meaning *against*) and *sub-* (meaning *under or below*).
- Give pairs of children A4 whiteboards and pens. Challenge them to invent new words, using at least two of the prefixes, and to write these words on their whiteboards along with brief definitions. You may wish to demonstrate this by writing up the word *superteacher* and asking the children to come up with a definition, e.g. 'The best teacher in the school.'
- Once they have completed the activity, ask each pair to join another pair and to share their new words and definitions. Take feedback from the activity, asking who has come across a new word that they think should become a real word. As a class, vote on their favourite new word and challenge the children to use it during the day.

5 Review

- Give each child a copy of the Prefixes resource (see You will need) and ask them to read it through and to think about possible missing words.
- Read the passage aloud, pronouncing the missing words clearly and giving the children time to write them in.
- Once they have finished the activity, give some time for the children to check their spellings and then ask each child to compare their spellings with a partner. Check whether there were any words that caused problems and re-visit these by writing them up and exploring strategies that the children find helpful in remembering spellings, e.g. visualising the word, saying each syllable clearly, emphasising unstressed vowels.

Prefixes

Klang steered his **submarine** carefully in an **anticlockwise** direction, nosing it into the cave below the cliff. He put a **refill** into his jelly gun and set off through the **subway** towards the superhero's lair. He could hear talking and laughter. 'A party!' he sneered, 'full of **superstars** I'll bet. Well, I am feeling rather **antisocial** tonight so I won't be joining in!'

The evil villain Klang had plotted his **return** carefully. His plan was to **replace** Superman as the world's greatest hero. But he did not realise that no one could step into the shoes of the man with the **superpower**. He was certainly heading for disappointment.

© 2016 Rising Stars UK Ltd.

Who will win the spelling quiz?
Focus: review of Spring term spellings

You will need:
Access online resources at My Rising Stars: www.risingstars-uk.com
- Group 1 focus word cards
- Group 2 focus word cards
- Group 3 focus word cards
- Group 4 focus word cards
- Group 5 focus word cards

In a nutshell
Teacher subject knowledge for this unit:
This unit gives the children a chance to use a range of strategies for learning, attempting and remembering how to spell a range of words that they explored during the Spring term units.

Word list

Group 1	Group 2	Group 3	Group 4	Group 5
famous	automobile	international	ball	groan
favourite	autograph	interview	bawl	grown
February	autobiography	interfere	berry	heel
forward	autocue	interrupt	bury	heal
fruit	automatic	interval	fair	vain
grammar			fare	vein
group			great	reign
guard			grate	rein
				rain

1 Introduce/Review

- Split the class into at least five groups and explain that they are each going to explore a spelling focus that they covered in the previous term. (If you would like the children to work in smaller groups, duplicate some of the sets of focus word cards, as appropriate.)
- Number the groups 1 to 5. Give each group their focus word cards (see You will need).
- Ask them to spread out their focus word cards on their tables and to read the words. Challenge them to work out what the spelling focus for their set of cards is.
- Ask each group to feed back to the rest of the class, summarising their spelling focus.
- Monitor the accuracy of their summaries, correcting any misunderstandings if they arise. Ask each group to write out their summaries and display these, along with examples of relevant words, on the working wall.

2 Teach

- Ask each group to carry out an Open word sort activity with their cards. Explain that they can choose how to group their cards but must be able to explain how and why they sorted them in a particular way.
- If any groups require support, remind them of other word sort activities they have done and the criteria they used, e.g. by spelling pattern; alphabetically by first, second and third letter; by number of syllables; by word class.
- Ask each group to feed back on their open sorting activity to the rest of the class, explaining how they sorted their words and why they chose that way of sorting them.

3 Practise

- Ask each child in the class to choose two words from their group focus words. You may wish to mediate the choices that some children make to check that the words are appropriate for the activity.

Summer term, Unit 2

Challenge!
Use the Spelling Fox Challenge: Who will win the spelling quiz? (3) to kick off or consolidate the learning. The children must help the Spelling Fox find the correct answers! Access online via My Rising Stars.

- Ask the children to work in their groups and to play Guess my word by giving clues about their words. If necessary, demonstrate this, giving clues about word meaning, initial and/or final letter sounds, spelling patterns contained in the word, number of syllables.
- If the rest of the group struggle to guess the word, they are able to ask questions but only receive yes or no answers.

4 Apply

- Ask each child to choose two different words from their group focus words.
- They should take it in turns to read their words aloud clearly and challenge the rest of their group to write them down, spelling them accurately.
- Once every child has read their words, they can spell them aloud, allowing the rest of the group to check the accuracy of their spelling.
- Ask the children to count up how many words they have spelled accurately and to record their score.

5 Review

- Within each group, give every child a number from 1 to 5 or 6, depending on the size of the group. Explain that all of the number 1 children will work together, all of the number 2s will work together, etc.
- Ask each child to choose two words from their group focus words and to take them to their new group.
- Once the new groups have formed, every group member should teach the rest of the group their words, including any spelling rules or conventions.
- Each group can then carry out a quick-fire spelling activity where every child reads out their two words at some speed while the rest of the group writes them down.
- Ask the children to count up how many words they have spelled accurately and to record their score. They can then add it to their score from the previous activity.
- Explore the range of scores that they have achieved, discussing with higher scorers what techniques they used to help them to spell accurately.

Who can remember the word list?
Focus: words from the Year 3/4 word list

You will need:
Access online resources at My Rising Stars: www.risingstars-uk.com
- Focus word cards
- Mind the gap resource per child

In a nutshell
Teacher subject knowledge for this unit:

The focus for this unit is on words taken from the statutory word list for Year 3/4. In addition to the well-established 'look, say, cover, write, check' strategy, the children can use techniques that incorporate a range of learning styles, e.g. identifying the tricky bits of words, visualising the word and specific spelling patterns, pronouncing the words clearly and emphasising the syllables, chanting the spelling aloud, using actions, drawing images.

Word list				
heard	heart	height	history	imagine
important	increase	interest	island	knowledge

1 Introduce/Review

- Write up the following words:

heard	height	imagine	increase	island
heart	history	important	interest	knowledge

- Read the words aloud to the children, pronouncing them clearly, and explain that these are the words they are going to focus on in this unit.
- Focus on *heard* and *heart* and ask the children to identify the common spelling pattern in the words ('ea'). Are they able to hear that the letters are pronounced differently in these [words?] up the words, spelling them aloud as you do so. Ask the children to read

[...] *istory* and *interest*. Then reread them, breaking the words down and [emphasising the] pronunciation: *his-tor-y*, *in-ter-est*. Write up the words, spelling them [aloud. Ask the chil]dren to repeat the words, again emphasising the pronunciation.

- Focus [on the wor]ds *height*, *island* and *knowledge*, reading each one aloud and pronouncing [them clearly. Cha]llenge the children to spot the letter sounds in the words that cannot be [heard when they] are read or spoken aloud, e.g. the 'gh' in *height*, the 's' in *island*, the 'k' in [*knowledge*. Write] up the words, spelling them aloud as you do so. Ask the children to read

[...Give the chil]dren the focus word cards (see You will need) and ask them to sort the [word] in any way that they choose. Once they have completed the word sort, [ask them to expl]ain how they have grouped the words, why they chose those groupings [and what they h]ave learned about the words.

[...the foc]us word list and read the words aloud together. Check that the children are [pronouncing the] words accurately and clearly.

[...] of focus words and read the first five (*heard*, *heart*, *height*, *history*, [*imagine*),] pronouncing them clearly. Ask the children to read them aloud with you. [Ask which p]arts of the words might be tricky to spell, e.g. the 'ea' in *heard* and *heart*, [the 'gh' in *hei*]*ght*.

[...im]*agine*, pronouncing it clearly. Ask what sound they can hear in the word [that isn't repre]sented by a letter (/dge/). Establish that the /dge/ sound is made by the [...] word.

60 © 2016 Rising Stars UK Ltd.

Summer term, Unit 3

Challenge!
Use the Spelling Fox Challenge: Who can remember the word list? (1) to kick off or consolidate the learning. The children must help the Spelling Fox find the correct answers! Access online via My Rising Stars.

- With the children, develop and write up five sentences that contain the focus words, e.g.
   a) I woke up when I heard the alarm.
   b) I felt my heart beat faster as the mysterious figure came closer.
   c) When I stand next to my best friend, you can see the difference in our height.
   d) In history we learn about what happened in the past.
   e) Just imagine what would happen if we could travel back in time.
- Ask them to read the sentences, focus on the words, then close their eyes and picture the words.
- Involve the children in spelling the five focus words aloud without looking at them. Write up the words and ask them to check whether they are spelled correctly.
- Repeat this process with the rest of the focus words. Once all of the words are written up correctly, read through the list, pronouncing them correctly, then reread them, accentuating the tricky parts of the words.

3 Practise

- Ask the children to work in pairs and choose three or more of the focus words for this unit. Explain that they are going to create dictionary entries for each of their words.
- Show an example of a dictionary entry and identify the features they should include, e.g. headword, word class, definition, example of a sentence containing the focus word.
- Choose one of the focus words and demonstrate how to create a dictionary entry for the word.
- Give the children time to create their own dictionary entries. Ask each pair of children to share their dictionary entries with another pair. Encourage them to comment constructively on each other's entries.
- Ask the children whether they need to make any changes to their entries given the feedback they have received. Once they are happy with their entries, they can write them on large sheets of paper for display on the working wall or in their word books or spelling journals.

4 Apply

- Give each child a copy of the Mind the gap activity (see You will need). Ask them to read the clues and fill in the gaps in each word with the correct letters. The letters in the shaded boxes will make a word from the focus word list.
- Once they have completed the activity, they can compare their answers with those of a friend.
- Establish whether there are any particular words, or parts of words, that are proving problematic and re-visit these. Write them up and, as a class, read each word and spell it aloud. Repeat this, increasing the pace each time.

5 Review

- Identify any words that the children are finding challenging.
- As a class, play Shannon's game, encouraging them to think about, and visualise, the spelling patterns in the words.
- Ask them to write the focus words in their word books or spelling journals and to check the accuracy of their spellings.
- Ask them to work with a partner. They should each choose five words from the focus word list and take it in turns to challenge their partner to spell the words aloud. They can repeat this until they can both spell the words correctly.

How does 'happy' become 'happily'?
Focus: the *-ly* suffix

You will need:
Access online resources at My Rising Stars: www.risingstars-uk.com
- Focus word cards
- A4 whiteboards and pens
- The Lazy Cat resource per child

In a nutshell

Teacher subject knowledge for this unit:

The focus for this unit is adding the suffix *-ly* to words. Adding this suffix turns adjectives into adverbs. When the suffix *-ly* is added to a word with more than one syllable that ends in the letter 'y', the 'y' changes to an 'i', e.g. *happy + -ly = happily*.

Word list

| happy | angry | easy | fussy | funny | greedy | merry |
| crazy | heavy | hungry | guilty | noisy | lazy | busy |

1 Introduce/Review

- Write up the following words:

  happy   angry   easy   fussy   funny   greedy

- Read them aloud to the children.
- Involve the children in using the words in sentences to establish understanding of the meanings, e.g.
    a) I was happy when our school team won the match.
    b) It makes me angry when I hear people being nasty to each other.
    c) It was easy to climb up the tree.
    d) My sister is fussy about what she eats.
    e) My dad thinks he is very funny when he tells jokes.
    f) Our greedy dog ate the cat's food as well as his own.
- Establish that in the sentences the focus words give more information about the nouns.
- Challenge them to tell you what word class the focus words belong to. (*adjectives*)
- Ask the children to work in pairs and to discuss what they all have in common in terms of spelling. (*They end in 'y'.*) Take feedback and agree that all of the words end in 'y'.

2 Teach

- Remind the children of work they have done on adverbs, explaining that adverbs can tell us how something is said or done.
- Demonstrate this by using the idea of the first sentence from the previous session in dialogue that uses an adverb, e.g. '"We won the match!" I shouted happily.' Write up the sentence.
- Involve the children in turning the second sentence into dialogue that includes an adverb, e.g. '"Don't be nasty to each other," I said angrily.' Write up the sentence.
- Ask them to identify the adverbs that have been formed from the adjectives (*happy – happily; angry – angrily*).
- Challenge them to spot the changes in spelling – the 'y' at the end of the words has been replaced by *-ily*.
- Write up the following words:

  shy   dry   bad   mad

- Demonstrate than when *-ly* is added to these words, the 'y' at the end of the word does not change to 'i', e.g. *shyly, dryly, badly, madly*.
- Challenge the children to spot the difference between the words *happy, angry, shy, dry, bad, mad*. If necessary, guide them towards counting the syllables in the words.

Summer term, Unit 4

Challenge!
Use the Spelling Fox Challenge: How does 'happy' become 'happily'? to kick off or consolidate the learning. The children must help the Spelling Fox find the correct answers! Access online via My Rising Stars.

- Establish that when the suffix *-ly* is added to a word with more than one syllable ending in 'y', the 'y' changes to an 'i'. Write this up and display it on the working wall, along with examples of words, e.g. *happy + -ly = happily*.
- Re-visit the rest of the sentences from the previous session and involve the children in turning the adjectives into adverbs by adding *-ly* and following the spelling rule.

3 Practise

- Ask the children to work in pairs. Give each pair a set of focus word cards, an A4 whiteboard and a pen.
- Ask them to choose three of the words and turn them into adverbs by adding *-ly* and following the spelling rule of changing the 'y' to an 'i', then adding the *-ly* suffix.
- They can write the adverbs on their whiteboards. Ask the children to hold them up so that you can check the accuracy of the spellings.
- Ask them to write down sentences that use their adverbs to demonstrate that they understand the meaning of each word.
- Take feedback from the activity, asking some pairs to read out their sentences. Encourage the rest of the class to comment on whether the sentences help them to understand the meanings of the words.

4 Apply

- Remind the children of the spelling focus for this unit.
- Explain that they are going to take part in a Speedy spelling activity.
- Give each child an A4 whiteboard and pen.
- Read out a selection of up to ten words from the focus words cards. As you read each word, ask the children to turn them into adverbs by adding the *-ly* suffix and making any necessary changes to the root words. They can then write the words on their whiteboards and hold them up so that you can check the spelling.
- Keep the activity fast paced.

5 Review

- Ask the children to remind you of the spelling focus for the unit and the rule that they have learned.
- Give a copy of The Lazy Cat resource (see You will need) to each child. Read the passage aloud, asking them to write in the missing words, checking that they are spelling them correctly.

    The Lazy Cat

    The cat stretched **lazily** in front of the fire. Suddenly, a mouse ran **speedily** across the room. The cat licked his lips **hungrily**. 'I could **easily** catch that mouse,' he thought **greedily**. The mouse stopped and **happily** nibbled the large piece of cheese that he was carrying. **Noisily**, the cat yawned and the mouse scampered off. 'But I won't try catching him today. That cheese is too smelly!' said the cat **fussily**.

© 2016 Rising Stars UK Ltd.

How does 'simple' become 'simply'?
Focus: the -ly suffix

You will need:
Access online resources at My Rising Stars: www.risingstars-uk.com
- A4 whiteboards and pens
- Focus word cards
- The Loose Tooth resource per child
- What am I? resource

In a nutshell

Teacher subject knowledge for this unit:

The focus for this unit is adding the -ly suffix to words. When a word ending in -le is turned into an adverb, the suffix -ly is added but the 'e' at the end of the root word is dropped.

Word list				
simply	humbly	crumbly	wobbly	bubbly
idly	gently	tickly	freckly	prickly
sparkly	twinkly	wrinkly	muscly	sensibly
cuddly	fiddly	giggly	wriggly	drizzly
horribly	possibly	terribly	responsibly	probably

1 Introduce/Review

- Before the lesson, write up these words in two columns as shown:

gentle	humbly
simple	gently
humble	horribly
sensible	sensibly
horrible	simply

- With the children, read the two lists aloud, checking they are pronouncing the words clearly.
- Ask them to work in pairs and to discuss with their partners anything they notice about the words in the two columns – what they have in common, what the differences are.
- Take feedback, encouraging them to support their observations with examples from the word lists. Establish that the words in the left-hand column are all adjectives and end in -le, whereas the words in the right-hand column are all adverbs and end in -ly.
- Ask whether they notice any connections between the two word lists. Involve individual children in matching up the words in each list.
- Give ten children an A4 whiteboard each and ask them to write down one of the words from the lists. Ask those with the words from the left-hand column to stand at the front of the class. Read each word aloud, asking the child with the connecting word to join their partner.
- Involve the rest of the class in reading the pairs of words, emphasising the -ly suffix at the end of the adverbs.
- Discuss how the spelling of each pair of words is different. Establish that when a word ending in -le is turned into an adverb, the suffix -ly is added. Reinforce that the 'e' is dropped.
- Write up two or three of the adjectives from the list and demonstrate how the spelling changes when they are turned into adverbs.

2 Teach

- Give an A4 whiteboard to each child and ask them to work in groups of six.
- Give each group a word from this list:

    wobble   tickle   cuddle   rattle   giggle

- Focus on one group at a time and ask individual children in the group to write one letter from the word on their whiteboards. They can then stand at the front of the class and form a 'living word'. Ask the rest of the class to check that the word is spelled correctly.

Summer term, Unit 5

Challenge!
Use the Spelling Fox Challenge: How does 'simple' become 'simply'? to kick off or consolidate the learning. The children must help the Spelling Fox find the correct answers! Access online via My Rising Stars.

- Challenge the rest of the class to turn the word into an adverb by writing the individual letters on their whiteboards. Remind them of the change to the word ending.
- Ask the class to use the word in a sentence to show that they understand what it means.

3 Practise

- Ask the children to work in groups of four or five. Give each child in the group a copy of the focus word list (see You will need). Point out that all of the words end in -ly and are organised in groups of five.
- Explain that they are going to do a Speedy spelling activity. Set up a timer to count down from a set time, e.g. one minute. Challenge them to read the first group of five words, remember as many of them as they can in the time given and then to hide the word list and write them down.
- Once they have written down the first group of words, they can check their individual spellings against the focus word list and record a group score.
- Each group can then repeat the activity with the second and subsequent groups of words, recording their cumulative group scores.
- Check the scores of each group and establish whether there are any particular words that the children are finding challenging. Re-visit these using the 'look, say, cover, write, check' approach until the children are more confident with the spelling of the words.

4 Apply

- Explain that you have found a piece of writing that is full of mistakes and that you need their help in correcting the spellings.
- Give each child a copy of The Loose Tooth resource (see You will need). Ask them to read though the passage and correct the words that the writer has got wrong. You could underline or highlight the incorrectly spelled words for some children, rather than leaving them to work them out for themselves.
- Take feedback, asking the children to tell you which words they have corrected, and how.
- Ask what advice they would give to the person who wrote the passage about how to correctly spell the words they got wrong.

> **The Loose Tooth**
>
> One **drizzley** Monday morning, I realised that I had a loose tooth. I **simppley** couldn't believe it! I **gentley** pushed it with my tongue. It was very **wobbley** and it hurt **horribbley**. My mum said I had to eat **crumbbley** food so that I didn't have to chew it. It was **terribley** difficult. Eventually, even though it was fiddley, I managed to pull my tooth out. The Tooth Fairy left me some money under my pillow which made me quite **giggley**!

5 Review

- Ask the children to remind you of the spelling focus for this unit, e.g. what happens when the suffix -ly is added to a root word that ends in -le.
- If necessary, remind them that most words ending in -ly are adverbs and that these words give more information about how something is done or what something is like.
- Tell them that they are going to do a What am I? activity (see You will need). You are going to read out some clues and the children should work out what the word is from the clues. You may wish to ask some children to have the focus word list to hand so that they can refer to it for ideas.

Can you correct your own writing?

Focus: words from children's own writing

You will need:
Access online resources at My Rising Stars: www.risingstars-uk.com
- Word books or spelling journals
- A4 whiteboards and pens

In a nutshell

Teacher subject knowledge for this unit:

This unit focuses on words that the children identify as incorrectly spelled in their own writing.

Following discussion on strategies for remembering how to spell specific words, the 'look, say, cover, write, check' approach is used to practise and reinforce spellings. The focus words are re-visited a number of times through various activities, giving the children the opportunity to read and reread the words, as well as writing them down and using them in sentences.

> **Word list**
> Identified by the children from their own writing.

1. Introduce/Review

- Ask the children to look through any writing they have done in English, and in other subjects, and to find up to ten words that they have spelled incorrectly. These may well be words that have already been identified by you during marking. Some children might need adult support in identifying these words.
- Ask them to draw up a 'look, say, cover, write, check' table in their word books or spelling journals and to write their focus words in the left-hand column. They should then check that they have spelled them correctly by asking a friend, an adult, reading the marking comments or checking in a dictionary.
- Ask them to work in pairs and to read their lists to each other, discussing what the words mean and which parts of the words they find particularly tricky to spell.

2. Teach

- As a class, discuss techniques that the children can use to remember spellings, e.g. pronouncing all of the letters in a word, including those that are silent; visualising whole words and letter patterns; spotting words within words; breaking words down into root words and prefixes/suffixes.
- Ask them to carry out the 'look, say, cover, write, check' process with each of the words on their lists, completing the table in their word books or spelling journals. You may wish to put a time limit on the activity to focus their attention on the task.
- Once they have completed their 'look, say, cover, write, check' tables, they can check with a partner that they have spelled the words accurately. If there is any dispute, they can check in a dictionary.

3. Practise

- Ask the children to re-present their original word lists as two separate columns: those they *did* spell correctly after the 'look, say, cover, write, check' approach, and those they *did not*. They could use a tick or a cross as the heading for the relevant list.
- Put the children into pairs, ensuring that between them they have some incorrectly spelled words. Challenge them to teach each other to spell the words on the incorrectly spelled list, using some of the strategies that they explored earlier in this unit. Make sure that the words originally spelled incorrectly are spelled correctly on the new list.
- Ask them to work in pairs and give each pair two whiteboards and pens. Explain that they are going to practise spelling their challenging words (the words they misspelled) by taking

Summer term, Unit 6

Challenge!
Use the Spelling Fox Challenge: Can you correct your own writing? (5) to kick off or consolidate the learning. The children must help the Spelling Fox find the correct answers! Access online via My Rising Stars.

it in turns to say a word and asking their partner to write it down on their whiteboard. They can then check the spelling against their word lists.
- As a follow up, they can read a word together and spell it aloud. Encourage them to develop a rhythm and build up speed with this so that it becomes a memorable chant.

4 Apply

- Ask the children to continue to work with their partners and to each choose five words from their original lists. They can then combine their words so that each pair has a collection of ten focus words.
- Challenge them to work together and to read and write the list of words, with the aim of reducing the number of incorrectly spelled words every time they go through the list. Some children might benefit from a time limit on the activity.
- At the end of the session, ask how many incorrectly spelled words each pair of children have left on their lists.

5 Review

- Ask the children to return to their own individual spelling lists created at the beginning of this unit and to swap them with a partner.
- They should read out each word on their partner's list, giving their partner time to write the words down correctly but maintaining a steady pace.
- Once each child has had the opportunity to write down their words correctly, they should check each other's lists.
- Finally, ask the children to develop and write sentences that include their focus words to show that they understand the meanings of the words.

How does 'basic' become 'basically'?

Focus: suffixes -ally and -ation

You will need:
Access online resources at My Rising Stars: www.risingstars-uk.com
- Matching pairs cards
- Change the word resource per child

In a nutshell

Teacher subject knowledge for this unit:

Adjectives can be turned into adverbs by adding *-ly*. Adjectives ending in *-ic*, e.g. *comic*, are turned into adverbs by adding the suffix *-ally*.

The *-ation* suffix turns verbs into nouns. If a root words ends in a consonant, the suffix is added to the end, e.g. *inform + -ation = information*. If the root word ends in an 'e', the 'e' is removed and the suffix is added, e.g. *prepare + -ation = preparation*. If the root word ends in a 'y', the 'y' is replaced by 'ic' and the suffix is added, e.g. *multiply + -ation = multiplication*.

Word list

basic	energetic	enthusiastic	admire	publish
basically	energetically	enthusiastically	admiration	publication
frantic	scientific	inform	sense	multiply
frantically	scientifically	information	sensation	multiplication
comic	terrific	prepare	determine	operate
comically	terrifically	preparation	determination	operation

1 Introduce/Review

- Remind the children of the work they did on turning words ending in *-le* into adverbs by adding the suffix *-ly*, e.g. *gentle – gently, terrible – terribly*. Establish that the 'e' in the root word is replaced with a 'y'.
- Write up these words:

    frantic   comic   energetic

- Challenge the children to tell you what spelling pattern they have in common. (*They end in -ic.*) Discuss the meaning of each of the words, establishing that they are adjectives.
- Are the children able to suggest how to turn them into adverbs? If necessary, remind them that adverbs often end in *-ly*. Experiment with some of the children's spelling suggestions by writing them up next to the root word. Discuss what 'looks' right in terms of the spelling.
- Write up the correct spelling of the three words:

    frantically   comically   energetically

- Discuss the suffix that has been added to make the adverb (*-ally*). With the children, write a summary of this spelling rule, e.g. 'To turn an adjective ending in *-ic* into an adverb, add *-ally*, e.g. *comic + -ly = comically*.' Display this on the working wall.
- Write up these words:

    inform   prepare   multiply

- Ask the children which word class these words belong to. (*verbs*) They can test whether a word is a verb by putting *to* in front of it and checking whether it is something they could do.
- Explain that they are going to turn these verbs into nouns by adding a suffix. Explore whether any of the children can suggest a suitable suffix (*-ation*). Demonstrate how to add the *-ation* suffix to the root words.

2 Teach

- Return to the root words – *frantic, comic* and *energetic* – and the three new words (adverbs) – *frantically, comically* and *energetically*. Identify the suffix that has been added to make

Summer term, Unit 7

Challenge!
Use the Spelling Fox Challenge: How does 'basic' become 'basically'? to kick off or consolidate the learning. The children must help the Spelling Fox find the correct answers! Access online via My Rising Stars.

- the adverb (-*ally*). Challenge the children to tell you what changes have been made to the spelling of the root word in order to turn it into an adverb. (*Adding the suffix -ally.*)
- Summarise this as a spelling rule, involving the children in the wording of the rule, e.g. 'Root words ending in -*ic* have the suffix -*ally* added when they are turned into adverbs.' You may wish to introduce the word *public*, which is the exception to this rule as it is spelled *publicly* when turned into an adverb.
- Focus on the root words (verbs) – *inform*, *prepare* and *multiply* – and the three new words (nouns) – *information*, *preparation* and *multiplication*. Discuss the changes that happen to the spelling of the root word, e.g. *inform* – *inform**ation*** (*straightforward adding of the -ation suffix*); *prepare* – *prepar**ation*** (*the final 'e' is dropped*); *multiply* – *multipli**cation*** (*the 'y' becomes 'ic'*).
- Write up these words:

  admire   sense   operate

- Ask the children to work in pairs and work out how they can turn these verbs into nouns by adding the suffix -*ation*. (*The final 'e' is dropped.*) Write up the correctly spelled nouns (*admiration, sensation, operation*).

3 Practise

- Ask the children to work in pairs. Give each pair a set of Matching pairs cards (see You will need). You may wish to give some children a limited number of the cards, e.g. a maximum of five pairs.
- Ask them to spread the cards, face down, on the table. The first child picks up a card, reads it aloud and then turns over another card. If it matches their card, i.e. it is the root word and the adverb (*in the case of -ally*) or the root word and the noun (*in the case of -ation*), they keep the pair and repeat the process. If the card they turn over does not make a pair, the other player has a go. The winner is the player with the most pairs of cards.
- Ask some of the winning children to feed back on the techniques they used in the game.

4 Apply

- Ask the children to work in pairs to sort the Matching pairs cards (see You will need) into two groups: root words and 'new' words (words with suffixes added).
- Ask them to each choose five words from the 'new' word pile. This could be a deliberate or random selection. The children can then work individually to compose orally, and then write, five sentences that each include one of their chosen words. Challenge some children to use two or more of the words in one sentence.
- Take feedback from the activity, checking with the rest of the class whether they think the focus words have been used appropriately in the sentences.
- Write up some of the sentences they have produced that include adverbs. Explore the word order in these sentences, demonstrating that the adverb can go in different places.

5 Review

- Give each child a copy of the Change the word activity (see You will need).
- Explain that they should read sentences a) to e) and change the word in the brackets to an adverb by adding the suffix -*ally*. With sentences f) to j), they should change the word in the brackets to a noun by adding the suffix -*ation*.
- Ask them to share their sheets with a partner and to compare their spelling of the words.
- Check whether any of the spellings caused any problems. If there are particular words that need to be re-visited, carry out a class or individual 'look, say, cover, write, check' activity.

How does 'control' become 'controlled'?
Focus: suffixes (vowel letters)

You will need:
Access online resources at My Rising Stars: www.risingstars-uk.com
- Focus word cards
- Suffix cards
- Goldilocks and the Three Bears resource per child
- Goldilocks and the Three Bears (answers) for display

In a nutshell

Teacher subject knowledge for this unit:

In words that end in a consonant, the final consonant is doubled when a suffix starting with a vowel is added *if* the stressed syllable is at the end of the root word, e.g. *control* + *-ed* = *controlled*. In words that end in a consonant, the final consonant is not doubled when suffixes starting with a vowel are added *if* the stressed syllable is at the beginning of the word, e.g. *visit* + *-ing* = *visiting*.

Word list

| forget | begin | prefer | garden | limit | control |
| cover | defer | occur | thunder | vandal | visit |

1 Introduce/Review

- Ask the children to tell you what they know about syllables. Point at yourself and say your name, clapping out the syllables. Ask them to identify how many syllables you clapped out. Point at individual children in the class, asking them to clap out the syllables in their names and the rest of the class to identify the number of syllables clapped out. Ask who had the most number of syllables in their name.
- Write up the following words:

    forget   begin   garden   limit

- Read each word, pronouncing it clearly and emphasising the stressed syllable in each case, e.g. for**get**, be**gin**, **gar**den, **lim**it. Ask them if they could hear that you said one part of each word more strongly. Involve them in underlining the stressed syllable in each word.
- Write up further words (*control, visit, thunder, admit*) and repeat the activity, underling the stressed syllable in each word, e.g. con**trol**, **vis**it, **thun**der, ad**mit**. Encourage the children to read the words with you and then ask some to read them individually. Check that they can both hear and reproduce the stressed syllable in the words.

2 Teach

- Return to the list of words produced during the previous session and write them up:
    for**get**, be**gin**, **gar**den, **lim**it, con**trol**, **vis**it, **thun**der, ad**mit**
- Give the suffix cards to some children, checking that more than one child has each suffix.
- Write up the following suffixes: *-ing, -ed, -en, -ation, -er, -est*.
- Point to and say the word *forget*. Ask who has a suffix that could be added to the word to make a new word. Those children can hold their suffix cards up. The rest of the class should check against the suffixes that you have written up.
- Write up the words that can be formed by adding suffixes to the word *forget*, e.g. *forgetting*. Explore how the root word changes if the suffix *-en* is added, e.g. *forgotten*.
- Repeat this activity with the following words: *begin, control, admit*.
- Ask them to think about what happens to the final letter in the root word once the suffix is added. (*It is doubled.*)
- Repeat the activity with the following words: *garden, limit, visit, thunder*.
- Ask them to explore what happens to the spelling of the root word when the suffix is added. (*Nothing – the final consonant is* not *doubled.*)

Summer term, Unit 8

Challenge!
Use the Spelling Fox Challenge: How does 'control' become 'controlled'? to kick off or consolidate the learning. The children must help the Spelling Fox find the correct answers! Access online via My Rising Stars.

- Ask the children what the words where the final consonant is doubled have in common. (*The stressed syllable is at the end of the root word.*) Ask what the words where the final consonant is not doubled have in common. (*The stressed syllable is at the beginning of the word.*)
- Write up these spelling rules and display them on the working wall along with some examples, e.g. 'In words that end in a consonant, the final consonant is doubled when a suffix starting with a vowel is added *if* the stressed syllable is at the end of the root word, e.g. *control* + *-ed* = *controlled*. In words that end in a consonant, the final consonant is not doubled when suffixes starting with a vowel are added *if* the stressed syllable is at the beginning of the word, e.g. *visit* + *-ing* = *visiting*.'

3 Practise

- Remind the children of the spelling rules established in the previous session.
- Give pairs of children sets of the focus word cards and the suffix cards (see You will need).
- Ask them to sort the focus word cards into two groups: those where the first syllable is stressed and those where the final syllable is stressed.
- Ask them to find a suffix that can be added to each root word to make a new word.
- Once they are happy with their suffix choices, they can collaborate in working out the spelling of the new words, based on the spelling rules from the Teach section.
- Ask some of the children to tell the rest of the class the words they have come up with and how they have spelled them. Write them up so that the whole class can see and decide whether the spelling is accurate.
- Check whether they think that the spelling rules have been followed.

4 Apply

- Remind the children of the spelling focus for this unit and, if necessary, re-visit the spelling rules displayed on the working wall.
- Give each child a copy of the reading passage (see You will need) and allow them time to read it through.
- Read the Goldilocks and the Three Bears passage aloud to them, saying the missing words clearly and allowing them time to write them in the space provided.

5 Review

- Carry out a Speedy spelling activity around the class with some of the focus words. Start by saying the focus word and the initial letter yourself. The child closest to you says the next letter in the word. The child next to them says the next letter, and so on, until the word is complete.
- As each child says a letter, write it up so that the whole class can see the word being spelled. Once the word is finished, ask them to check the spelling and make any necessary changes. Repeat this activity with other focus words.

How does 'confuse' become 'confusion'?

Focus: -*sion* and -*tion* endings

You will need:
Access online resources at My Rising Stars: www.risingstars-uk.com
- Focus word cards
- The Director's Cut resource per child
- The Director's Cut (answers) for display

In a nutshell

Teacher subject knowledge for this unit:

Verbs can be changed into nouns by having the /shun/ sound added to the end, e.g. *confuse* (verb) – *confusion* (noun). When following this convention, words ending in 't', lose the 't' and have the suffix -*tion* added, e.g. *correct* + -*tion* = *correction*. Words ending in 'de' lose the 'de' and have the suffix -*sion* added, e.g. *collide* + -*sion* = *collision*.

Word list

divide	tense	complete
decide	televise	invent
explode	expand	inject
collide	extend	act
persuade	comprehend	divert
confuse	hesitate	

1 Introduce/Review

- Write up these words:

    action   explosion   decision   invention

- Read them aloud to the children. Ask them to read the words aloud to each other, listening carefully to the sounds in the words.
- Challenge them to identify a sound that each word contains (/shun/). Ask where this sound is in each word. (*At the end.*)
- Ask what they notice about the letters at the end of each word that make the /shun/ sound. (*They are either* -sion *or* -tion.)
- As a class, identify the root word in each /shun/ word, e.g. *act, explode, decide, invent*. Write up these root words, drawing the children's attention to the fact that some of the words change slightly in their spelling when they are root words.
- Ask them what they notice about the final letters in the root words. (*They end in 't' or 'de'*.) Together, work out that words ending in 't' lose the 't' and have the suffix -*tion* added and words ending in 'de' lose the 'de' and have the suffix -*sion* added.
- Check whether they are able to identify that the root words are verbs and the /shun/ words are nouns.
- Formulate these conventions as spelling rules and display them on the working wall along with some examples of words that conform to these rules, e.g. 'Verbs can be changed into nouns by having the /shun/ sound added to the end, e.g. *confuse* (verb) – *confusion* (noun). When following this convention, words ending in 't' lose the 't' and have the suffix -*tion* added, e.g. *correct* + -*tion* = *correction*. Words ending in 'de' lose the 'de' and have the suffix -*sion* added, e.g. *collide* + -*sion* = *collision*.'

2 Teach

- Re-visit the spelling rules displayed on the working wall. Remind the children how the spelling of the root words changes when the suffixes are added.
- Write up these words:

    expansion   confusion   tension   extension   hesitation   completion

Summer term, Unit 9

Challenge!
Use the Spelling Fox Challenge: How does 'confuse' become 'confusion'? to kick off or consolidate the learning. The children must help the Spelling Fox find the correct answers! Access online via My Rising Stars.

- Involve the children in identifying the letters that make the /shun/ sound at the end of the words. Challenge them, in pairs, to write down the root word in each word (*expand, confuse, tense, extend, hesitate, complete*).
- Establish that when the root words end either in 'de', 'd' or 'se', these final letters are removed and the suffix *-sion* is added when the root words are turned into nouns. When the root words end in 'te', these final letters are removed and the suffix *-tion* is added. Add this information to the spelling rules created earlier, e.g. 'Words ending in 't' or 'te' lose these final letters and have the suffix *-tion* added. Words ending in 'de', 'd' and 'se' lose these final letters and have the suffix *-sion* added.' Display this information on the working wall.
- Establish that the root words are verbs and the /shun/ words are nouns.

3 Practise

- Re-visit the spelling rules created earlier, asking the children to give you some examples of verbs that take a /shun/ ending when turned into nouns.
- Ask them to work in pairs and give each pair a set of focus word cards. You may wish to give some pairs fewer words. Ask them to draw up two columns on a sheet of paper and to write the headings *-tion* at the top of one column and *-sion* at the top of the other.
- The children should read each word card, orally turn it into a noun by adding a /shun/ ending and then decide which suffix it would take and place it under the correct heading.
- Once they are happy with the position of their word cards, they can write out each word, spelled correctly, under the relevant heading.
- Ask each pair to join up with another pair to check the spelling of their words. If they have any incorrectly spelled words, ask them to note these down and think about strategies they could use to help them to remember how to spell them, e.g. visualising the shape of the word, saying each syllable/letter sound clearly.

4 Apply

- Ask the children to work in pairs. Give each pair a set of focus word cards. Ask them to familiarise themselves with the words.
- Remind them of the spelling focus for this unit. Ask them to work in pairs and to use the cards to come up with an activity or game that will help them to remember the spelling rules about adding the /shun/ sound to the end of a word.
- Once the children have developed their activity, they can share it with another pair.
- Take feedback, asking how they feel that their activities would help them to learn and remember the spelling rules.

5 Review

- Ask the children to remind you of the spelling focus for the unit and to give you some examples as illustrations.
- Give each child a copy of The Director's Cut resource (see You will need) and ask them to read it through.
- Explain that you are going to read the passage aloud to them and that they should write in the missing words, checking their spellings carefully.

   The Director's Cut

   As I ran through the darkness, I came to a **division** in the path. I stopped. I knew I had to make a **decision** about which way to go. There was no time for **hesitation** so I sprang into **action**. I turned right. Suddenly, I heard the sound of an **explosion**. There was a **collision** of colours and sounds and I fell to the ground in **confusion**.
   'Cut!' called the director. I rolled over, **tension** draining from my body. I'd done it. I'd just filmed my first **television** appearance and I knew that it wouldn't be my last!

How does 'active' become 'inactive'?

Focus: *in-* and *il-* prefixes

You will need:
Access online resources at My Rising Stars: www.risingstars-uk.com
- Focus word cards
- Dictionaries
- Change the word resource per child

In a nutshell

Teacher subject knowledge for this unit:

Prefixes are groups of letters that can be added to the beginning of a word. They usually change the meaning of the root word. The prefixes *in-* and *il-* mean *not* and turn a root word into a negative. When a root word starts with 'l', the prefix used to turn the word into a negative is *il-* rather than *in-*.

Word list				
inactive	incorrect	incapable	indirect	invalid
inaccurate	inaudible	illegal	illegible	illiterate

1 Introduce/Review

- Explain to the children that the focus for this unit is prefixes. Ask them to tell you what they know about prefixes. (*They are a group of letters added to the beginning of words; they change the meaning of words.*) Are they able to give you some examples of prefixes and words with prefixes?
- Write these down, involving individual children in identifying the root words and prefixes. Discuss the meanings of the root words and the words with prefixes.
- Write up the following words:

    correct   active

- Discuss the meanings of these two words, asking the children to help you to put them into sentences, e.g. 'My teacher said that we all had to try to get our spellings correct. We try to be active at break by running around.'
- Ask them to discuss how to make words with the opposite meaning by adding a prefix. Demonstrate that adding the prefix *in-* to the root word produces a word with the opposite meaning, e.g. *incorrect, inactive*. Involve the children in creating sentences that include these two words, e.g. 'Unfortunately, all our spellings were incorrect so our teacher was not happy. We are really inactive at break because we don't run around at all.'
- Establish that the prefix *in-* means *not* and turns a root word into a negative.

2 Teach

- Re-visit the words with *in-* prefixes and ask the children to remind you what the *in-* prefix means. (*not*)
- Write up these words:

    legal   literate

- Discuss their meanings. Use them in sentences to help the children to understand the word meanings, e.g. 'The police officer said that it was legal to play on the swings during the day. Everyone in our school can read and write so we can say that we are all literate.'
- Challenge the children to spot what the two words have in common. (*They both start with 'l'*).
- Try saying the root words with the prefix *in-*, e.g. *inlegal, inliterate*. Establish that they are quite difficult to say and sound odd. Write up *illegal* and *illiterate*. Establish that when a root word starts with 'l', the prefix used to turn the word into a negative is *il-* rather than *in-*.

Summer term, Unit 10

Challenge!
Use the Spelling Fox Challenge: How does 'active' become 'inactive'? to kick off or consolidate the learning. The children must help the Spelling Fox find the correct answers! Access online via My Rising Stars.

3 Practise

- Ask the children to work in pairs. Give each pair a set of the focus word cards (see You will need). Ask them to read each of the words carefully.
- Ask them to spread their cards, face down, on the table in front of them. The first child picks up a card, reads it aloud and then turns over another card. If it matches their card, they keep the pair and repeat the process. If the card they turn over does not make a pair, the other player has a go. The winner is the player with the most pairs of cards.
- Take feedback from the activity and ask the children who successfully gathered a number of pairs to explain the strategies they used.

4 Apply

- Ask the children to remind you of the focus for this unit, e.g. using the prefixes in- and il- to make negative words. Explore their understanding of the meaning of the prefix (not).
- Ask each child to choose two or three of the focus words and to discuss their meanings with a partner.
- Explore their understanding of alphabetical order by asking them to arrange their words alphabetically. Check that they are clear that the second, third and even subsequent letters in a word are relevant when organising words alphabetically.
- Make sure that every child has access to a dictionary. Ask them to write down each of their words, then to look them up in the dictionary, record the meanings of the words and finally use them in a sentence.
- Ask them to share their definitions and sentences with a partner.
- Take feedback from the activity, checking the accuracy of their understanding of the words by focusing on the sentences that they have created.
- Home in on a small number of the focus words that the children are likely to come across in their reading and use in their writing. Involve them in writing sentences that use the words in a way that makes their meaning clear.
- Display these sentences on the working wall.

5 Review

- If necessary, re-visit the focus of this unit: adding the in- and il- prefixes to root words.
- Give each child a copy of the Change the word activity (see You will need). Explain that they should change the word in brackets in each sentence to a negative word by adding either the in- or the il- prefix.
- Once they have completed the activity, they can share their sheets with a partner and check whether they have created the same words.
- Ask each pair to develop a statement about which prefix to use, and why.

© 2016 Rising Stars UK Ltd.

How does 'possible' become 'impossible'?
Focus: *im-* and *ir-* prefixes

You will need:
Access online resources at My Rising Stars: www.risingstars-uk.com
- A4 whiteboards and pens
- Focus word cards
- Dictionaries
- Change the word resource per child

In a nutshell
Teacher subject knowledge for this unit:

Prefixes are groups of letters that can go at the beginning of a word. They usually change the meaning of the root word. The prefixes *im-* and *ir-* mean *not*, like *in-* and *il-*. When a root word starts with 'r', the prefix used to turn the word into a negative is *ir-* rather than *im-*.

Word list

immature	impolite	irregular	irresistible
impossible	imperfect	irrelevant	irresponsible
impatient	immobile	irrational	

1 Introduce/Review

- Give A4 whiteboards and pens to pairs of children.
- Ask them to discuss with a partner what they know about prefixes and to write down some examples on their whiteboards. Discuss the meanings of the prefixes and challenge them to give you examples of words that start with the prefixes.
- If necessary, remind them that the focus in the previous unit was on the prefixes *in-* and *il-*. Are they able to tell you what those prefixes mean and to give some examples of words that start with *in-* and *il-*?
- Write up these words:

    possible   polite   perfect

- Challenge them, in pairs, to write the meaning of at least one of the words on their whiteboards and to hold them up. Carry out a quick check of the definitions to monitor their understanding.
- Are they able to suggest how the words could be turned into words with the opposite meaning by adding a prefix? Write up their suggestions or guide them towards adding the prefix *im-*, e.g. *impossible, impolite, imperfect*.
- As a class, develop sentences that contain the new words.
- Establish that the prefix *im-* means *not*, like *in-* and *il-*. Write this up and display it on the working wall.

2 Teach

- Write up the prefix *im-* and ask the children to remind you what it means (*not*).
- Write up the following words:

    regular   responsible   relevant

- Discuss their understanding of these words.
- Together, develop sentences that include the words so that their understanding of their meanings is developed, e.g.

    a) A square is a regular shape with four sides and four corners.
    b) During the holidays, I was responsible for looking after the class pet.
    c) It is not relevant that I was there when the window was broken.

- Challenge them to spot what the three words have in common. (*They all start with 'r'*.)
- Try saying the root words with the prefix *im-*, e.g. *imregular, imresponsible, imrelevant*. Establish that they are quite difficult to say and sound odd. Write up *irregular, irresponsible* and *irrelevant*. Establish that when a root word starts with 'r', the prefix used to turn the word into a negative is *ir-* rather than *im-*.

Summer term, Unit 11

Challenge!
Use the Spelling Fox Challenge: How does 'possible' become 'impossible'? to kick off or consolidate the learning. The children must help the Spelling Fox find the correct answers! Access online via My Rising Stars.

- Read the words together and try using them in sentences to reinforce their meanings.
- Summarise the spelling rules explored so far and display them on the working wall, e.g. 'The prefixes *im-* and *ir-* mean *not*, like *in-* and *il-*. When a root word starts with 'r', the prefix used to turn the word into a negative is *ir-* rather than *im-*.'

3 Practise

- Ask the children to work in small teams of four or five. Give each team a set of the focus word cards (see You will need). Ask them to familiarise themselves with the words by reading through the cards.
- Ask them to play Guess my word by each choosing one of the focus words and developing four or five clues about the word. You may wish to offer some suggestions, e.g. a clue could give information about the number of syllables in the word, the meaning, the first/final letter.
- Each team member gives their team five marks and then reads out their clues, one by one. For every wrong answer, or non-answer, the team loses a mark. The next team member has their go, again giving the team five marks to start with. Ask the teams to keep track of their marks. The team with the most marks at the end is the winner.
- Ask the winning team to share their winning strategies with the rest of the class.

4 Apply

- Ask the children to remind you of the focus for this unit, e.g. using the prefixes *im-* and *ir-* to make negative words. Explore their understanding of the meaning of the prefix (*not*).
- Ask each child to choose two or three of the focus words and to discuss their meanings with a partner.
- Explore the children's understanding of alphabetical order by asking them to arrange their words alphabetically. Check that they are clear that the second, third and even subsequent letters in a word are relevant when organising words alphabetically.
- Make sure that every child has access to a dictionary. Ask them to write down each of their words, then to look them up in the dictionary, record the meanings of the words and finally use them in a sentence.
- Ask them to share their definitions and sentences with a partner.
- Take feedback from the activity, checking the accuracy of their understanding of the words by focusing on the sentences that they have created.
- Home in on a small number of the focus words that they are likely to come across in their reading and use in their writing. Involve the children in writing sentences that use the words in a way that makes their meaning clear.
- Display these sentences on the working wall.

5 Review

- If necessary, re-visit the focus of this unit: adding the *im-* and *ir-* prefixes to root words.
- Give each child a copy of the Change the word activity (see You will need). Explain that they should change the word in brackets in each sentence to a negative word by adding either the *im-* or the *ir-* prefix.
- Once they have completed the activity, they can share their sheets with a partner and check whether they have created the same words.
- Ask each pair to develop a statement about which prefix to use and why.

Who can remember the word list?

Focus: review of Year 3 words from the Year 3/4 word list

You will need:
Access online resources at My Rising Stars: www.risingstars-uk.com
- Word lists 1–5
- Bean bags or small balls
- A4 whiteboards and pens
- Anagrams resource per child

In a nutshell

Teacher subject knowledge for this unit:

The focus for this unit is on reviewing the words from the statutory word lists for Year 3/4 that the children have covered during Year 3. The activities use visual, kinaesthetic and auditory activities to re-visit and embed spelling knowledge.

> **Word list**
> Word lists 1–5 are included in the online resources (see You will need).

1 Introduce/Review

- Ask the children to work in teams of five.
- Explain that you are going to read a list of words aloud and that they should each write them down, thinking carefully about the correct spelling of every word, without discussing the spelling with their team mates.
- Read word list 1 to the children, pronouncing the words clearly. Once you have read all of the words and they have written them down, involve the children in spelling the words aloud accurately. Write up the correctly spelled words and ask them to check their own spellings and to add up their team's score, giving one mark for each correct spelling.
- Record the number of marks that each team have scored on a team scoreboard.
- Discuss the challenges they had when they were trying to spell the words. If necessary, explore some techniques and strategies they could use to help them the next time, e.g. visualising the word, visualising the tricky part of the word, saying the word syllable by syllable, thinking about root words.

2 Teach

- Focus on the problem words from word list 1. Explore some of the typical misspellings from the previous activity and support the children in correcting their spellings.
- Write up or display word list 2. Read the words aloud to the children and then ask them to read the words to the person sitting next to them. Remove or hide the word list.
- Give each team five lives. Play Shannon's game with one of the words from the list by writing up the initial letter followed by an appropriate number of dashes representing the rest of the letters in the word.
- Remind the children to think about what letters can and cannot follow on from previous letters. Take suggestions for possible letters from each team in turn.
- If a suggestion is incorrect, the team loses a life. The team with the most lives left at the end of the round is the winner.
- Keep a record of the number of lives each team has left. Repeat this with other words from the list, giving each team five lives every time you focus on a new word.
- Add the overall number of lives each team has to their original score on the team scoreboard.

3 Practise

- Focus on any words from word list 2 that the children found challenging. Discuss the challenges they had when they were trying to spell the words. If necessary, explore some techniques and strategies they could use to help them the next time, e.g. visualising the word, visualising the tricky part of the word, saying the word syllable by syllable, thinking about root words.

Summer term, Unit 12

Challenge!
Use the Spelling Fox Challenge: Who can remember the word list? (2) to kick off or consolidate the learning. The children must help the Spelling Fox find the correct answers! Access online via My Rising Stars.

- Write up or display the words from word list 3. Read the words aloud to the children and ask them to read them chorally in their teams. Take the class to an open area such as the hall or playground. Give one member of each team a bean bag or small ball, appoint a scribe for each team and give that child an A4 whiteboard and pen.
- Ask each group to sit in a circle. Explain that they are going to play Letter tennis. Say one of the focus words aloud. The child holding the bean bag or ball says the first letter in the word, the scribe writes the letter down. The bean bag or ball is passed to another team member and they say the next letter in the word and the scribe writes it down. This is repeated until the teams have spelled the word.
- Spell the word aloud to the children, asking the scribes to check their team's spelling. Award one mark for a correctly spelled word. Keep track of the teams' marks and add them to their existing scores on the team scoreboard.

4 Apply

- Focus on any problem words from word list 3. Explore some of the children's typical misspellings and support them in correcting their spellings.
- Write up or display the words from word list 4. Read the words aloud and then ask the children to read them aloud to their neighbour. Hide or delete the list.
- Ask them to work in their teams and give each team two or three copies of the Anagrams resource (see You will need). If necessary, explain that an anagram is a word with the letters mixed up.
- Challenge the teams to sort out the anagrams and write out the words correctly spelled. They can share out the anagrams and work individually or in pairs within their teams. Once they have worked out the word, they can write it, correctly spelled, on their sheets. At the end of the activity, ask teams to swap their sheets and check the spellings of the words against word list 4.
- Add the number of marks scored by each team to their existing score on the team scoreboard.

5 Review

- Write up or display the words from word list 5. Read the words aloud to the children, asking them to repeat them after you.
- Ask them to stand up and explain that they are going to create an action to help them to remember each word. Point to and read the word *heard*, spell it aloud and add an appropriate action, such as cupping your hand to your ear.
- Ask them to read the word, spell it aloud and copy the action. Repeat this with the rest of the words, re-visiting the words you have covered every so often to reinforce the actions.
- Once actions have been created for all of the words, point to words in word list 5 at random, asking the children to read the words, spell them aloud and do the actions.
- Delete or cover up word list 5. Give each team an A4 whiteboard and pen. Say the words on word list 5, ask the children to spell them aloud, write them down and do the actions.
- Reveal word list 5, ask each team to check their spellings and award one mark for every correct spelling.
- Add the teams' scores to their existing scores on the team scoreboard. Declare an overall winner of the Year 3 team spelling challenge.